MADE IN GO

The Catholic Vision of Human Dignity

Edited by
Regis Duffy, O.F.M.
&
Angelus Gambatese, O.F.M.

PAULIST PRESS
New York / Mahwah, N.J.

Cover design by Moe Berman

Copyright © 1999 by the Province of the Most Holy Name (O.F.M.)

Library of Congress Cataloging-in-Publication Data

Made in God's image : the Catholic vision of human dignity / edited by Regis Duffy & Angelus Gambatese.
    p. cm.
   Includes bibliographical references.
   ISBN 0–8091–3850–6 (alk. paper)
    1. Dignity—Religious aspects—Catholic Church. 2. Sociology, Christian (Catholic) 3. Catholic Church—Doctrines. I. Duffy, Regis A. II. Gambatese, Angelus.
BX1795/D55M33   1999
233′.5—dc 21   98–40531
                                                   CIP

Published by Paulist Press
997 Macarthur Boulevard
Mahwah, New Jersey 07430

www.paulistpress.com

Printed and bound in the
United States of America

Contents

Introduction

Regis Duffy, O.F.M., and
Angelus Gambatese, O.F.M.

The evening news has a way of making abstract terms come alive. Hunger, for example, can remain an undisturbing idea until we see the face of a starving child in Africa on the television. The same is true of "human dignity" until we see the victims of rape or violence or hear the heated debates about the rights of illegal aliens. Affronts to human dignity form a major part not only of televised or printed news, but also of the lives of many people within our borders. Human dignity, then, is the multifaceted reality that forms the background of life and death in America and resists any facile definition.

This book does not start with a definition of human dignity but immediately suggests specific problems and attitudes that legitimize the regular attacks on human dignity, even by those who consider themselves committed Christians. Behind these various discussions lurks the question that one of our contributors, James S. Dalton, articulates in his article: Why should human beings have importance and what accounts for this importance? Put differently, why should we feel affronted by televised or printed accounts of the flagrant disregard for human dignity unless we hold human beings sacred, both for their gifted natures and for their privileged destinies.

The Christian response to Dalton's question has developed over the centuries as a result of grappling with specific cultural and historical problems that called into question the practicality of living the gospel message. If a theologian, for example, wished to develop a Christian response to the problem of slavery, it would seem a fairly straightforward project: God has created all equal and Christ died for all—slavery ignores and violates these basic tenets of Christianity and is therefore evil. But slavery in Paul's time and in Bartolomé de Las Casas's time

1

also had specific sociocultural configurations that complicated both the theological response and the lived ethic of the gospel. The gospel challenge to live a life of service in love is betrayed when the specific historical and sociocultural contexts are minimized or dismissed.

This book attempts to respect and to profit from the complex contexts of the question of human dignity. It is the result of an interdisciplinary process that fostered a dialogue among a group of scholars. Thanks to the generous support of the Bonfils Foundation of Denver, Colorado, and the Franciscan Friars of Holy Name Province, they met three times during the course of two years. This diverse group of scholars brought their own perspectives, honed by their particular disciplines, to the question of human dignity. Initial generalizations and assumptions about human dignity, understood within a Christian perspective, gradually became a clarifying dialogue, more sharply focused by concrete case studies. From this process a series of draft papers emerged. These were exchanged among the participants for critical reaction and discussion at subsequent meetings. As a result of this collegial dialogue and eventual consensus, these papers reflect a thoughtful commentary on and contribution to the Christian perspective on human dignity.

In the initial article, "Creation-Incarnation: God's Affirmation of Human Worth," James P. Scullion provides an appropriate biblical context for the discussion of human dignity by asking, What is the covenantal meaning of human worth? By carefully examining the creation stories of Genesis, he uncovers an important "coherent theme," the creation of human beings in the image and likeness of God. Scullion finds a second theme in the incarnation that renews and intensifies this divine likeness in human beings. A powerful counterpoint to this theme are the ways in which the prophets Jesus and Paul make use of contingent situations in which to apply these themes. But, the author insists, these same themes cry out for appropriation in our own specific life-situations.

The title of James Dalton's article outlines his topic: "Human Dignity, Human Rights, and Ecology: Christian, Buddhist, and Native American Perspectives." His initial question, cited earlier, is worth repeating: "Why should human beings have importance and what accounts for this importance?" Once this question is asked within a specific culture and tradition, however, its multivalent character is revealed. Although the answer to this question in Western Christianity has taken different and even divergent paths through the centuries, there is a certain evolving continuity and concern about human rights as an expression and test of human dignity. A sharp contrast to this world-view is provided by Buddhism where all is seen as impermanent. This perspective, however, allows for an ecology and appreciation of human rights because in every situation relationships are necessary. Although it is difficult to generalize about Native American views, we can say that human dignity, in their perspective, is linked to the cosmic order of being and, in particular, to nature. The tragic story of the displacement of Native Americans with their separation from their sacred places is but one example of the violation of human dignity. Dalton suggests intriguing possibilities for a dialogue between these three world-views and how this might enrich our practice of human dignity and rights as well as a responsible ecology.

Is there a mentality, call it commodity-consciousness, that threatens human dignity as insidiously as the more blatant forms of violence and hate? Ron DiSanto answers affirmatively in his chapter, "The Threat of Commodity-Consciousness to Human Dignity." Commodity-consciousness includes not only the insatiable acquisition of things and the purchasing power to do so but also the tendency to regard human beings as commodities to be bought and sold. DiSanto proposes love-consciousness, richly understood as both agape and eros, as an antidote to this disease. Love-consciousness restores our priorities and perspective, allowing us to acknowledge the goods worth pursuing and their place in a well-ordered life. DiSanto then examines three dynamics in a capitalist world—the profit motive, competition, and employment practices—and demonstrates how they can minimize human dignity. Love-consciousness, in response to such dangers, calls for right views, right attitudes, and right speech.

Edward Foley begins his contribution, "Preaching about Dignity or Preaching with Dignity," with a short but effective case study of a Sunday morning homily. Foley is not interested in repeating the frequently heard charges of irrelevance and boredom of such homilies. Rather, he argues persuasively that liturgical preaching "is a critical, self-defining activity in which the church publicly models and rehearses what it genuinely believes about the dignity of the baptized and, by implication, the dignity of other human beings as well." The liturgical homily, like all liturgical celebration, provides for an encounter between God and the assembly. God again uncovers the connections between the fabric of our lives and the purposes of God's saving action in them. Our dignity (and that of others) is reinterpreted and appropriated in such encounters. But the experience of the listening assembly is both key to and object of such preaching. Foley offers a practical strategy for preaching with dignity that respects and interprets such experience.

In "Immigration Reconsidered in the Context of an Ethic of Solidarity" Patricia A. Lamoureux tackles the difficult problem of rights language and its reconceptualization so as to deal with current problems of immigration. She draws upon the tradition of Roman Catholic social teaching of the past one hundred years in order to propose a language of solidarity as the context for the teaching on human rights. What emerges from a close reading of this teaching is the inadequacy of rights language of itself to deal with the threats to human dignity. But an ethic of solidarity demands a fundamental attitudinal change toward others, especially those who are unable to defend themselves. Lamoureux draws a set of conclusions from this ethic that are demanding but evangelical.

Robert J. Wister adds another pressing issue to this collage on human dignity in "Fragile Outcasts: Historical Reflections on Ministry to Persons with AIDS." He begins with a historical situation that might seem far removed from a discussion of AIDS ministry—the flagrant abuses against the human dignity of the native populations of the Americas. The sad outcome of that story contrasts sharply the story of Catholic healthcare in this country and the challenge it has encountered in the spiritual and physical care of AIDS patients. Many AIDS patients have been separated from institutional religion for a number of years because of the judgmental attitudes they had found there. Wister recounts one successful ministerial response to these fears, the Chrysalis Ministry, which provides non-denominational retreats for people with AIDS. In much the same spirit displayed by de Las Casas, Chrysalis affirms the human dignity of these people through these days of spiritual affirmation and healing.

There is a unifying plea underlying all these themes, the need for a radical re-evaluation of our priorities and a consequent change in our praxis in regard to things and to people, especially those who have been marginalized by more affluent societies. The Christian insistence on human dignity only attains its full voice when each generation assumes the responsibility of applying this principle to its own situations and value system. Lamoureux sums up this unifying theme when she describes the ethic of solidarity as "an ethic of character that has to do with the kind of people we are and hope to become."

This theme, in turn, indicates the audience to whom this book is directed. The contributors to this work are christian scholars who not only write about human dignity but are concerned with its practice. They address themselves to all educated readers and especially to those in ministry who want to explore how the gospel command to find Christ in the imprisoned and impoverished might find expression in their own situations and times. Although this examination of human dignity has benefited from the Roman Catholic tradition and its social teaching, it is hoped that it will also serve Christians of other traditions and all who wish to deepen their appreciation of human dignity.

Our hope is that this book might further sensitize readers to the questions of human dignity and enable them to contribute the ongoing conversation about and the actual healing of the human indignities of our time.

Creation-Incarnation:
God's Affirmation of Human Worth

James P. Scullion, O.F.M.

Violence mars the landscape of city and country: the countries of Bosnia-Herzegovina, Rwanda, Northern Ireland, Lebanon, and Israel have all become symbols of horrific and senseless violence. Reports of violence in our cities are commonplace: one day newspapers report the story of a mother murdering her child after months of abuse and the next day the story of a mother breaking down in tears as she is told that her teenage son has just been murdered in a drive-by shooting. Whether one looks at the near or the distant past, one sees people of violence and innocent victims of violence, particularly women and children.

The experience of violence is not one any of us can hide from. It is an experience that we need to reflect upon because it not only mars the landscape of city and country, it mars our human dignity as well. This chapter will reflect theologically upon human dignity and the experience of violence. Theological reflection brings our tradition, our life experience, and our culture into a creative dialogue (Whitehead, 1995, 6–12). This essay will focus on our tradition, specifically the Sacred Scriptures, as a normative source for reflection on human dignity and for crafting a pastoral response to the epidemic of national and international violence.

Sacred Scripture contains what can appear to be a bewildering and at times contradictory array of prescriptions, proscriptions, exhortations, and narratives. In order to respect this diversity as well as the integrity of the Word of God the coherence-contingency model developed by J. Christiaan Beker (Beker, 1984, 11–16) can provide a helpful guide to explore the biblical foundations for human dignity. Coherence focuses on the underlying theological center while contingency explores the particular and diverse expressions of this center.

This coherent center will be located in the twin themes of creation

7

and incarnation. The creation story affirms the dignity of human beings since they are created in the image and likeness of God. This creation story is retold in the redemptive experience of the exodus and in the new creation of the return from exile. The incarnation expresses and reaffirms human worth through the Word becoming human flesh. While this coherent theme runs throughout the Bible, there is also a counter-theme of violence, violence caused by God and the elect of God. This challenge to the coherent center raises important hermeneutical issues that must be explored.

The particular and contingent expressions of this twin center (creation-incarnation) will be explored in the prophetic, the Synoptic, and the Pauline literature. The prophets, including Jesus, challenged those (especially the powerful) who tried to falsify the story of creation by denying the dignity and worth of the marginal (e.g., widows and orphans, outcasts and sinners). Finally Paul's application of this creation/new creation theme will be explored in his letters written to deal with particular issues in specific churches.

This survey will attempt to highlight these evocative and formative themes which can guide our modern reflection on human dignity and suggest a pastoral response to the proliferation of violence. The Bible itself models how to apply these coherent themes to contemporary contingent situations.

I. COHERENT CENTER

It is important to first sketch out a coherent center that underlies the diverse narrative *(haggadah)* and legal *(halakah)* interpretations in the Old and New Testaments. While the themes that will be explored are not found in every book of the Bible, they are found in all sections of the Jewish and Christian canons. What we are searching for is a "focal image," a particular imaginative characterization or lens through which to view the whole of the Scripture (Hays, 1996, 194–95).

A. Torah—Affirmation of Human Dignity

The Jewish canon is divided into three sections: Law *(Torah)*, Prophets *(Nebi'im)*, and the Writings *(Ketubim)*, hence the acronym

TaNaK. The most important section of the canon is the Torah, a source of delight for Jews:

> Happy are those who do not follow the advice of the wicked,…but their delight is in the Torah of the LORD, and on his Torah they meditate day and night. They are like trees planted by streams of water, which yield their fruit in its season, and their leaves do not wither. In all that they do, they prosper. (Ps 1:1–3)[1]

Meditation on the Torah has led and continues to lead Jews and Christians to a deeper understanding of God and of themselves. Thus in seeking the coherent or theological center of the Hebrew Bible we must begin with the Torah.

1. The First Creation Story: Genesis

The first book of the Torah called Genesis by Christians and *Bere'shit* ("In the beginning") by Jews provides a rich storehouse for meditation and reflection. The climax of the first creation account is the creation of human beings: "So God created humankind in his image, in the image of God he created them; male and female he created them" (Gn 1:27). The narrator indicates stylistically that the creation of human beings forms the climax of this story of creation. Six times the narrator emphasizes the goodness of creation: "And God saw that it was good…" (*kî tôb,* 1:4, 10, 12, 18, 21, 25). The seventh time, after the creation of human beings, the narrator highlights the superlative goodness of creation: "God saw everything that he had made, and indeed, it was very good" (*kî tôb me'od,* 1:31; cf. Sir 49:16).

Scholars have proposed various interpretations of the phrase "image and likeness" (1:26, 27). The two terms refer to (1) the natural and supernatural likeness; (2) the spiritual qualities or capacities; (3) the external or corporeal form; (4) humans as God's representative or viceroy; (5) the person as a whole, particularly as a counterpart of God (Westermann, 1984, 147–58). This last wholistic interpretation probably catches the meaning best. Since human beings as a whole are created in God's image and likeness they are able to enter into relationship and partnership with God.

This creation story forms the basis for the affirmation of human dignity. A. A. Di Lella calls it the "the charter statement of human dignity and equality of all men, women, and children in the sight of God" (Di Lella and Skehan, 1987, 282, 280). While God "forms" inanimate and animate beings, and "creates and blesses" living creatures and humankind (1:21–22, 27–28), only human beings are created in God's "image and likeness" (Gn 1:27–28; cf. Wis 2:23; Sir 17:3). As Wolfhart Pannenberg suggests: "Rightly, then, the Christian tradition sought the basis of personal dignity in our creation in the image of God (Pannenberg, 1994, 176).

The book of Genesis is important not only for what it says about human dignity but also for what it says about violence. Those who choose the way of violence are not imaging God. The word *image* appears four times in the book of Genesis (1:26–27; 5:3; 9:6), *likeness* three times (1:26; 5:1, 3). After 1:26–27 the phrase *image and likeness* does not occur again until chapter 5, the narration of the birth of Seth who is begotten in the likeness and image of Adam:

> When God created *adam,* he made them in the *likeness* of God. Male and female he created them, and he blessed them and named them adam when they were created. When Adam had lived one hundred thirty years, he became the father of a son in his *likeness,* according to his *image,* and named him Seth. (5:1–3)

As God created humankind *(adam)* in the divine image and likeness (1:26–27; 5:1–2) and named them *adam,* so Adam begot a son in his image and likeness and named him Seth (5:3; cf. 9:6). Significantly the narrator refuses to describe Cain, the one who committed fratricide by killing his brother Abel, as created in the divine image and likeness. Seth, not Cain, is the one who perpetuates the divine likeness (Williams, 1991, 25).

The second and third section of the Jewish canon, the Prophets *(Nebi'im),* and the Writings *(Ketubim)* can be viewed as the continuance of Torah instruction: the prophetic books call Israel to be faithful to the Torah and challenge it when it is not. The Writings are meditations on the Torah. For example, the psalmist marvels over this creation story:

> What are human beings that you are mindful of them, mortals that you care for them? Yet you have made them a little

lower than God, and crowned them with glory and honor.
You have given them dominion over the works of your
hands; you have put all things under their feet.... (Ps 8:4–7)

To be created in the "image and likeness of God" (Gn 1:26, 27) means to
be a little lower than God, crowned with glory and honor. Glory is the
visible or felt presence of God. Like the book of Genesis, the psalmist
also affirms the dignity of human beings as creatures "crowned with
glory and honor. "

The book of Wisdom, a book outside the Jewish but within the
Roman Catholic canon, provides another commentary on creation in
God's image. The Greek translation of the Hebrew Bible uses the word
eikon to translate the Hebrew word *selem* ("image"). Human beings are
icons of God. Wisdom explains what it means to be an icon of God:
"...God created us for incorruption, and made us in the image *(eikon)* of
his own eternity, but through the devil's envy death entered the world,
and those who belong to his company experience it" (Wis 2:23–24). The
book of Wisdom affirms that human beings have a dignity similar to
God's since like God they were created to be immortal.

The creation story in Genesis 1 and the commentaries on this story
in Psalm 8 and Wisdom 2 show us one of the underlying coherent centers
of the OT, namely, the dignity of humanity. Creation in the image and
likeness of God forms the basis of this human dignity. In turn, this creation story is retold and developed in the stories of the exodus and exile.

2. The Second Creation Story: Exodus

The second book of the Torah, the book of Exodus, is really the
second story of creation, specifically the creation of Israel. Scholars
have begun to emphasize once again the close connection between the
story of creation and the story of the exodus. As Terence E. Fretheim
notes:

> Exodus must be interpreted as the second chapter of a drama
> begun in Genesis...the themes of creation, promise, and
> universal divine purpose, set in place by the Genesis narra-
> tive, constitute lenses through which Exodus is to be read.
> (Fretheim, 1996, 229–30)

The story of the exodus is the foundational story of Israel's formation and redemption, a story that is intimately connected to the story of creation. The structure of Exodus binds it to Genesis 1–9. Fretheim suggests the following connections (1996, 231):

1. a creational setting (Ex 1:7; cf. Gn 1:28)
2. anti-creational activity, especially violence
3. Noah and Moses (Ex 2:1–10; 33:12–17; cf. Gn 6:8)
4. the flood and the plagues as ecological disasters
5. death and deliverance through water, with cosmic implications
6. covenant

The story of the exodus is connected to both the creational setting of Genesis 1 and the anti-creational activity of Genesis 4. As in Genesis 4, violence is anti-creational: people of violence, oppression, and infanticide (Ex 1:11–14) refuse to recognize the dignity of human beings. While the story of creation established the dignity of all humanity, since they are created in the divine image and likeness (Gn 1:26–28), the story of the exodus establishes the special dignity of the Israelites. They are redeemed, freed from their dehumanizing slavery in Egypt. They are a people God has chosen to be his own (Dt 7:6; 14:2).

3. The Third Creation Story: Deutero-Isaiah

As the exodus story is closely connected to the creation story in Genesis 1, so the story of the return from exile is bound to the story of creation and exodus. The prophet who forecast the return from exile, Deutero-Isaiah, combines the themes of creation and exodus (Stuhlmueller, 1990, 335):

> But now thus says the LORD, he who *created* you, O Jacob, he who *formed* you, O Israel: Do not fear, for I have *redeemed* you; I have *called you by name,* you are mine. When you pass through the waters, I will be with you; and through the rivers, they shall not overwhelm you; when you walk through fire you shall not be burned, and the flame shall not consume you....Because you are precious in my sight, and honored, and I love you, I give people in return for

you, nations in exchange for your life. Do not fear, for I am with you; I will bring your offspring from the east, and from the west I will gather you. (Is 43:1–5)

The Lord who created (44:2, 21, 24) and redeemed Israel (41:14; 43:14; 44:6, 22–24; 48:17; 49:7) promises ransom and repatriation (Whybray, 1981, 83). This second book of Isaiah (chaps. 40–55) pictures this return as a new creation. R. N. Whybray (Whybray, 1981, '82) comments:

> In using in this way verbs [created, formed] which were normally reserved for statements about the creation of the world, Deutero-Isaiah was asserting that Israel has a unique place in the divine order of things. At the same time, by speaking of what were normally thought of as *redemptive* acts in terms of creation, he was making it possible for the *new* redemptive acts of which he was about to speak to be regarded as nothing less than a new creation. Once again the Lord affirms the dignity of Israel: "...you are precious in my sight, and honored, and I love you." (43:4)

Genesis affirms the dignity of humankind in the story of creation. This story is reimaged in the key events of Israel's history, the exodus and exile. Thus, creation, specifically the creation of human beings in the image and likeness of God, serves as a pervasive and coherent theme in the Old Testament. Our examination of three "creation stories" has led to the discovery of one of the coherent centers in the Sacred Scripture.

B. Jesus—Reaffirmation of Human Dignity

Jesus, like his fellow Jews, delighted in the Torah and meditated on it day and night (Ps 1:2). We have seen that creation forms one of the underlying theological themes of the Torah. This theme highlights the dignity of human beings who are created in the image and likeness of God. Jesus recognized the divine dignity of all people, especially the outcasts of his society, lepers (Mk 1:39–45; 14:3), toll collectors (Mk 2:15–17), and Samaritans (Jn 4:4–42). If the story of creation affirms the dignity of humanity, the story of the incarnation reaffirms and focuses that story.

1. The Story of the Incarnation: John

Toward the end of the first Christian century the author of the gospel of John reflected in his prologue on the meaning and purpose of the creation story in Genesis ("In the beginning..." Gn 1:1; Jn 1:1) as well as of Jesus' incarnation:

> In the beginning was the Word, and the Word was with God, and the Word was God. He was in the beginning with God. All things came into being through him, and without him not one thing came into being....And the Word became flesh and lived among us, and we have seen his glory, the glory as of a father's only son, full of grace and truth....From his fullness we have all received, grace upon grace. The law indeed was given through Moses; grace and truth came through Jesus Christ. No one has ever seen God. It is God the only Son, who is close to the Father's heart, who has made him known. (Jn 1:1–3, 14–18)

Just as the creation story affirms the dignity of humanity, so the incarnation, the Word becoming flesh, reaffirms and even intensifies this dignity. As Gail O'Day suggests: "The incarnation binds Jesus to the 'everydayness' of human experience. When the believing community confesses...that the Word 'lived among us,' it affirms the link between the incarnation and its own humanness" (O'Day, 1995, 526). Jesus in his incarnation reveals God's glory, that is, the felt or visible presence of God. Jesus can do this because he is the one who is "close to the Father's heart" (Jn 1:18). The incarnation affirms human worth through the Word becoming human flesh: "...through the Incarnation, the Logos enabled us to be partakers of the divine sonship" (Schnackenburg, 1968, 266). So God is present in the human sphere (Brown, 1966, 35). The incarnation, therefore, exalts the dignity of humanity.

2. The Story of the Cross: Paul's Gospel

Like Jesus before him, Paul came to a deeper understanding of God and humanity through his meditation on the Torah. Paul also brought the story of the cross (1 Cor 1:18) into this meditation. This story of the cross tells the story of redemption ("...justified by his grace as a gift, through the redemption that is in Christ Jesus," Rom 3:24) and new creation ("So if anyone is in Christ, there is a new creation: everything old has passed away; see, everything has become new," 2 Cor 5:17). As we have seen, the creation theme of Genesis is retold and reimaged as redemption in Exodus and new creation in Deutero-Isaiah. Paul likewise reimaged the story of the incarnation (Phil 2:6–8) and the cross (1 Cor 1:18) as redemption (Rom 3:24; 8:23; 1 Cor 1:30) and new creation (2 Cor 5:17; Gal 6:15). So J. Christiaan Beker, linking the themes of creation and redemption, argues that the coherent center of Paul's gospel is "the proleptic fulfillment of the triumph of God, that is the redemption of the created order" (Beker, 1984, 351; Hays, 1996, 19–27).

The story of the cross also unmasks the deceit of violence by exposing the victimization mechanism of scapegoating (Lv 16:20–22; Rom 3:25; 2 Cor 5:21). James G. Williams, applying the insights of René Girard, suggests that "[the] Gospels' story of Jesus as the innocent Victim reveals the fate of the God...whose presence in the world so threatens and subverts structures of violence that it cannot be tolerated" (Williams, 1991, 12; Girard, 1979, 1986).

C. Conclusions

The first part of this chapter sought a coherent center in the Sacred Scripture. This underlying theological center was found in the twin themes of creation and incarnation. The story of the creation of humanity is the key: creation in God's image and likeness establishes the dignity of all human beings. This creation story was retold in the story of the exodus and the story of the return from exile. These two stories are formative stories for the Israelites (exodus) and the Jews (exile).

The second theme, the incarnation, is closely aligned to the theme of creation found throughout the OT. If creation in the divine image and likeness is the charter statement of human dignity then that charter has been renewed and intensified through the incarnation, God becoming a human being.

II. COUNTER-THEME

As any casual reader of the Bible is aware, it is at times a violent book. The coherent center that I have described does not form the whole story: not only does the Bible mention "wars and rumors of wars" (Mk 13:7), it also pictures God's elect fighting a "holy war" led by God, the divine warrior. This picture is offensive, even scandalous, to many today (Hobbs, 1989, 208–33; Miller, 1965, 40–41). Yet how does one deal with such images when they are contained in normative sources? After a survey of the OT and NT description of God as divine warrior and the so-called holy war, we will need to face the hermeneutical issue: are these images normative for our theological reflection

A. God, the Divine Warrior

The image of God as divine warrior is found throughout the Bible. God is celebrated as the triumphant warrior from the oldest hymn in the Bible, the Song of Miriam (Ex 15:21), to the last book of the Bible, Revelation (19:11–21). The Song of Moses proclaims: "The LORD is a warrior; the LORD is his name. Pharaoh's chariots and his army he cast into the sea; his picked officers were sunk in the Red Sea" (Ex 15:3–4). The King of Glory is "the Lord, strong and mighty, the Lord, mighty in battle" (Ps 24:8). As warrior, God serves as Rock, Fortress, Deliverer; he rides on a cherub, sends out his arrows, scatters and routes the enemies of Israel (Ps 18:2, 10, 14). The prophets warn, however, that this divine warrior could attack even Judah and Israel for their injustice: "For three transgressions of Judah, and for four...I will send a fire on Judah and it shall devour the strongholds of Jerusalem" (Am 2:4–5; cf. Dt 13:12–16; Jer 20:11).

The image of God as divine warrior also appears in the NT. The seer John reports the following vision concerning God or the Word of God:

> Then I saw heaven opened, and there was a white horse! Its rider is called Faithful and True, and in righteousness he judges and makes war....And the armies of heaven, wearing fine linen, white and pure, were following him on white horses. From his mouth comes a sharp sword with which to

strike down the nations, and he will rule them with a rod of iron; he will tread the wine press of the fury of the wrath of God the Almighty. (Rv 19:11–15)

The "armies of heaven" are the chosen and faithful ones. These armies of the holy ones led by the divine warrior crush and destroy the enemies, the Romans. The Romans replace the Egyptians and Canaanites as the enemies of God and his elect.

Like the prophet Amos, the seer John warns that this divine warrior could war against the elect, the church in Smyrna: "Repent then. If not, I will come to you soon and war against them with the sword of my mouth" (Rv 2:16).

B. Holy War and *Herem* (Ban/Annihilation)

Closely aligned with the image of God as warrior is the concept of "holy war" or YHWH's war (von Rad, 1991; Hobbs, 1989, 199–207). The book of Numbers refers to a book called the "Book of the Wars of the Lord" (Nm 21:14; cf. 1 Sm 18:17), which apparently described some of these "holy wars." War was looked upon as a sacral institution that required purity on the part of the soldiers (Jos 3:5; Dt 23:9–14). The cult object par excellence, the Ark of the Covenant, often led the warriors into battle (Jos 3:11).

At times as part of these "holy wars" the total annihilation *(herem)* of the population of the conquered city was called for:

But as for the towns of these peoples that the LORD your God is giving you as an inheritance, you must not let anything that breathes remain alive. You shall annihilate them— the Hittites and the Amorites, the Canaanites and the Perizzites, the Hivites and the Jebusites—just as the LORD your God has commanded, so that they may not teach you to do all the abhorrent things that they do for their gods, and you thus sin against the LORD your God. (Dt 20:16–18)

Israel is instructed to show no mercy as they carry out the *herem* (Dt 7:2; Jos 11:20). This "orgy of destruction" (Lohfink, 1986, 194) is also found in the Isaiah's prophecy against Edom (Is 34:1–15).

The concept of "holy war" and the image of God as divine warrior were not unique to Israel but reflected the culture and ideology of its time (Brettler, 1993, 135–36). For example, in the Moabite Mesha inscription (ninth century B.C.E.) the God Chemosh commands the total annihilation of the Israelite population of Nebo. Similar parallels can be found among the Greeks, Romans, Celts, Germans, and Arabs (Lohfink, 1986, 189–91; Miller, 1965, 42).

C. Hermeneutical Issues

Commenting on these OT texts, Patrick Miller suggests that the wars of YHWH pose historical, theological, and apologetic problems: "historical in terms of the history of the institution of holy war and the ban, theological in terms of the Old Testament understanding of God, and apologetic in terms of the incompatibility of these wars with the basic aspects and characteristics of the Christian faith" (Miller, 1965, 41). Wilfrid Harrington sees these hermeneutical issues not only in some OT texts but also in some NT texts, specifically the book of Revelation:

> There is...an unsavory side to the wielding of divine power....Violence comes from the One on the throne, and from the Lamb. The "wrath" of God is emphasized, a wrath poured out in a series of increasingly destructive plagues. There is a vindictiveness, underlined at the close of the vintage scene (14:17–20)....Or, again, the gruesome feast prepared for birds of prey (19:17–18) in a battle generalled by the Lamb! (Harrington, 1993, 24–25)

We cannot lightly dismiss these images since they are found from the beginning of the Bible (Exodus) to the end (Revelation). One needs, however, to assess the consistency and authority of these images.

We have seen that there is a coherent theme running through both the testaments that underlines the dignity of all humanity. Violence was seen as an affront to this dignity. Richard Hays in an important recent book on the moral vision of the NT also emphasizes the pervasiveness of this theme: "...from Matthew to Revelation we find a consistent witness against violence and a calling to the community to follow the example of Jesus in *accepting* suffering rather than *inflicting* it" (Hays, 1996, 332).

Hays also proposes some methodological guidelines to help us to deal with the contradictory voices in Scripture (Hays, 1996, 309–10). Applying those guidelines to the issue of violence in the Bible, he argues that "the New Testament witness is finally normative. If irreconcilable tensions exist between the moral vision of the New Testament and that of particular Old Testament texts, the New Testament vision trumps the Old Testament" (Hays, 1996, 336). Yet we have seen that it is not only OT texts but also NT texts that seem to espouse violence and depict God as warrior. So the tension is not just between the moral vision of the NT and the OT but within the testaments themselves.

Four points can be made to further refine the approach of Hays: (1) This martial language and imagery was not unique to the Israelites or the Christians. It was part of the culture and world-view of the time. As Christians we need not and should not unreflectively adopt this worldview or its language. (2) While the image of God as warrior and the theme of "holy war" is found in both the Old and New Testaments, it is not a central or coherent theme. The theme of "holy war," therefore, must be viewed and critiqued through the "focal image" of human dignity with its consequent rejection of violence. (3) The powerful image of Jesus, his nonviolent life and his death for others form the inner canon, or rule, by which Christians must judge these other peripheral images of divine warrior and "holy war." (4) Normative interpretation is a community process (Hays, 1996, 188–89). It seems that believing and praying communities are finding this bellicose language more and more problematic. In the light of these reflections I would judge the image of God as divine warrior and the theme of "holy war" not to be normative and probably not even helpful language to use in our theological reflection.

III. CONTINGENT INTERPRETATION

In the previous sections we saw how creation, and specifically the creation of humankind in God's image and likeness, formed at least one of the underlying theological centers of the Hebrew Scripture. This emphasis on human dignity is reinforced and intensified by the NT story of the incarnation. Now we want to see how this theological vision was applied and conditioned by contingent situations.

A. Prophets: The Concomitant Cry for Social Justice

In this section we will see how three prophets or pastoral theologians, Jeremiah (preexilic), Trito-Isaiah (postexilic), and Jesus, applied this coherent vision of human dignity to the contingent situations of their times. The second section of the Jewish canon, the Prophets *(Nebi'im),* is a commentary on or application of the Torah. While the Torah affirmed human dignity, the prophets called the people to particularize their recognition of this dignity through their compassion for the marginalized.

1. Jeremiah 7: The Temple Sermon

In the year 609 B.C., the accession year of King Jehoiakim, Jeremiah delivered his so-called Temple Sermon (Bright, 1965, 171–72, 57–59; Holladay, 1986, 249). The contingent situation is the seemingly miraculous deliverance of the Temple and Jerusalem from the siege of the Assyrian king Sennacherib (701 B.C.) that gave the people a false sense of security in the Jerusalem cult. The prophet proclaims his message at the entrance to the Temple. He warns the people not to trust in the Temple and its cult alone:

> The word that came to Jeremiah from the LORD. Stand in the gate of the Lord's house, and proclaim there this word, and say, Hear the word of the LORD, all you people of Judah, you that enter these gates to worship the LORD. Thus says the LORD of hosts, the God of Israel: Amend your ways and your doings, and let me dwell with you in this place. Do not trust in these deceptive words: "This is the temple of the LORD, the temple of the LORD, the temple of the LORD." (7:1–4)

In his call for repentance Jeremiah calls the people to recognize the dignity not just of God through their ritual observance but also of human beings through social justice:

> For if you truly amend your ways and your doings, if you truly act justly one with another, if you do not oppress the alien, the orphan, and the widow, or shed innocent blood in this place, and if you do not go after other gods to your own

hurt, then I will dwell with you in this place, in the land that
I gave of old to your ancestors forever and ever. (7:5–7)

Jeremiah calls the worshipers to recognize the dignity of all people, particularly the marginalized of society, the people with no voice, namely,
resident aliens, orphans, and widows. He calls the people to perform
deeds of righteousness, that is, "ameliorating the situation of the desti-
tute" (Weinfeld, 1995, 7, 220). Anachronistically we might say that Jeremiah calls the people to observe both the spiritual and the corporal
works of mercy. If the people fail to reform, Jeremiah threatens the
destruction of the Temple:

> Go now to my place that was in Shiloh, where I made my
> name dwell at first, and see what I did to it for the wicked-
> ness of my people Israel. And now, because you have done
> all these things, says the LORD, and when I spoke to you per-
> sistently, you did not listen, and when I called you, you did
> not answer, therefore I will do to the house that is called by
> my name, in which you trust, and to the place that I gave to
> you and to your ancestors, just what I did to Shiloh.
> (7:12–14. Cf. 26:4–6; Ps 78:60)

As a result of his Temple sermon Jeremiah was arrested, charged
with blasphemy and threatened with death by the priests and prophets
(26:7–11). He was spared only when the Jewish princes intervened and
argued for his release by pointing out that previously the prophet Micah
had prophesied the destruction of Jerusalem (3:12) and yet had been
spared by King Hezekiah (26:16–19).

Jeremiah concretizes the vision of the Torah. Since all human
beings are created in the divine image, the dignity of all human beings,
especially the resident alien, the orphan, and the widow, must be recognized and respected. It is not enough to trust in the Temple; one must act
as God acts by doing righteousness and justice.

2. Isaiah 58: The True Fast Day

The prophet conveniently called Trito-Isaiah prophesied after the
exile. Like Jeremiah before him and Jesus after him, the author of Trito-

Isaiah called for worship with justice. In a sermon perhaps delivered on the Day of Fasting, Yom Kippur (Weinfeld, 1995, 18, 142), the prophet attacks empty ritual:

> Shout out, do not hold back! Lift up your voice like a trumpet! Announce to my people their rebellion, to the house of Jacob their sins. Yet day after day they seek me and delight to know my ways, as if they were a nation that practiced righteousness and did not forsake the ordinance of their God; they ask of me righteous judgments, they delight to draw near to God. "Why do we fast, but you do not see? Why humble ourselves, but you do not notice?" (Is 58:1–3)

The people's claim to practice justice and righteousness (v. 2) is shown to be false: they have failed to recognized the dignity of their workers, the oppressed, the hungry, and the homeless.

> Look, you serve your own interest on your fast day, and oppress all your workers....Is such the fast that I choose, a day to humble oneself?...Will you call this a fast, a day acceptable to the LORD? Is not this the fast that I choose: to loose the bonds of injustice, to undo the thongs of the yoke, to let the oppressed go free, and to break every yoke? Is it not to share your bread with the hungry, and bring the homeless poor into your house; when you see the naked, to cover them, and not to hide yourself from your own kin? (Is 58:3–7)

The prophet effectively contrasts Israel's desire for ritual with the Lord's desire for compassion (Stuhlmueller, 1990, 345). The sins of the house of Jacob are their failure to recognize the dignity of the marginalized: "It meant forgetting that the God whom Israel worshipped was a God who takes the side of the oppressed....To worship Yahweh and to countenance injustice was, in fact, idolatry" (Hoppe, 1983, 44; cf. McKenzie, 1968, 166; Barré, 1985, 94–97). Recognition of the dignity of the marginalized meant the concrete acts of giving food to the hungry, drink to the thirsty, and shelter to the homeless.

3. The Sermon on the Mount: A Greater Righteousness

While Jesus can be viewed in many ways, from marginal Jew (Meier) to Mediterranean Jewish peasant (Crossan), almost all scholars involved in Jesus research have recognized the prophetic element in Jesus' life and ministry. Like Jeremiah, Jesus performed a prophetic action in the Temple (Mk 11:15–17; cf. Jer 7:1–15; 26:4–6) and threatened its destruction (Mk 13:1–2; cf. Jer 7:12–14; 26:6). This prophetic action eventually led to his arrest for blasphemy and a sentence of death (Mk 14:46, 63–64; cf. Jer 26:8, 16). Like both Jeremiah and Trito-Isaiah, Jesus called for a cultic life conjoined with social justice (Mk 12:28–33; Mt 9:13; 12:7; cf. Hos 6:6).

The author of the gospel of Matthew adapted Jesus' call for justice or righteousness to the situation in his own community, a predominantly Jewish community going through an identity crisis, a community that had experienced the destruction of the Temple and expulsion from the synagogue. Matthew tried to show this church (16:18; 18:17) how to be faithful to both the new, Jesus, and the old, Judaism (13:52).

In the programmatic beginning to the Sermon on the Mount Jesus calls his disciples to a fulfillment of the Torah (5:17–19) and to a greater righteousness (5:20). These two statements form the topics for the first half of the sermon (5:17—6:18). In a series of antitheses (5:17–19, 21–48) Jesus delineates what true fulfillment of the Torah entails: it rejects the way of violence (anger, vengeance, hatred) and injustice (adultery, divorce, false oaths). Jesus' call for a greater righteousness (Mt 5:20; 6:1–18) involves the nonhypocritical performance of cultic duties, specifically almsgiving (6:2–4), prayer (6:5–15), and fasting (6:16–18). Matthew emphasizes the importance of righteousness through its sevenfold use in his gospel (3:15; 5:6, 10, 20; 6:1, 33; 21:32). In the Sermon on the Mount, Matthew, like Jeremiah and Trito-Isaiah, shows that righteousness entails both cultic observance and social justice, that is the recognition of the dignity of both God and humanity.

B. Paul: "Be Who You Are"

Paul addressed his letters to specific communities in order to deal with particular and divergent issues in these communities. The structure of the Pauline letters reveals his pastoral approach to these issues: the body of his letters moves from a doctrinal section to a hortatory section (Fitzmyer, 1990, 770). In other words, Paul moves from the indicative, who they are, to the imperative, what they ought to do. His moral instruction can be neatly summarized: "Be who you are." The imperative follows from the indicative:

In dealing with contingent issues Paul asked the local communities to remember who they are. The believer is one who has been redeemed (Rom 3:24; 8:23; 1 Cor 1:30) and created anew (2 Cor 5:17; Gal 6:15). In Galatians, for example, when Paul deals with the specific issue of circumcision and its necessity for salvation he brings to bear this coherent overview: "For neither circumcision nor uncircumcision is anything; but a new creation is everything" (Gal 6:15). Paul's coherent center (new creation) guides him to a specific moral or pastoral decision, namely, circumcision is not required for Gentile male converts.

IV. CONCLUSION

The goal of theological reflection is not simply the clarification of a religious question but pastoral decision (Whitehead, 1995, 16). It is a model that "moves from a sympathetic listening to...these sources, through a constructively assertive dialogue generating insight, to a decision translating the theological insight into pastoral action" (Ulrich and Thompson, 1980, 31).

We have been engaged in a sympathetic listening to the Sacred Scripture. This listening has brought forward a coherent story, the story of the creation of humankind in the image and likeness of God, a story that would see violence as anti-creational activity. This story appears not only in the book of Genesis but also in Exodus, Isaiah, John, and Paul and indeed throughout the Bible. The counter-theme of "holy war," with God as the divine warrior, was also studied and ultimately rejected as a central and hence normative theme in the Bible. Finally, we looked at concrete examples in which the prophets, Jesus, and Paul applied this coherent theme of human dignity to contingent situations.

A full theological reflection on human dignity and violence would require that we listen also to the lived experience of the Christian communities as well as the voice of our culture. Nevertheless, this listening to the Scripture does begin to suggest some appropriate pastoral actions.

A. Modeling

The coherence-contingency model highlights powerful and evocative themes (creation and incarnation) that affirm the dignity of all human beings. This approach also "models" the application of these themes in specific and concrete situations. Sound pastoral praxis would call upon us to do likewise by making these themes central in the concrete situations of our celebrating, preaching, teaching, and living. It is less a need for information and more a need for people, especially the poor and marginalized, to experience their human dignity. Scripture challenges us to recognize the dignity of all human beings. Anything less would falsify the story of creation.

The prophets also challenge us to identify and condemn the subtle and not so subtle acts of violence in our society. As we have seen, violence is anti-creational whether it is oppression and infanticide (Ex 1:11–14) or anger, vengeance, and hatred (Mt 5:21–48). People of violence are not truly imaging God. Jesus' death on the cross revealed the victimization mechanism of scapegoating and the deceit of violence. We need to expose modern attempts to make scapegoats and the temptation to give in to this deceit of violence.

B. Better Stories: From Stories of Violence to Stories of Creation

What is one to do with Scripture? How is one to use it in moral decision making? Often the Bible has been mined for a list of do's and don'ts: "thou shalt...thou shalt not." A different and perhaps more helpful approach is to use the Bible in spiritual direction and character formation. A narrative approach to Scripture is very congenial to such a direction and indeed mirrors Jesus' own approach in his use of parables. Jesus' stories did not always give people a message; rather they gave people an experience, an experience of the Reign of God.

This essay has made frequent allusions to the story of creation because stories are not only important but also formative.

> Whoever can give his people better stories than the ones they live in is like the priest in whose hands common bread and wine become capable of feeding the very soul. (Kenner, 1971, 39)

The challenge, then, before us as pastoral ministers is to feed people's souls by giving them better stories than the ones they live in. Using the "focal image" or coherent theme of human dignity we can guide them in their reading of Scripture and in the process of finding their own story within the Scripture.

The story of the creation of humankind in the divine image and likeness is a better story than the story of a mother killing her child or the story of a mother weeping over a child slain in a drive by shooting. As pastoral ministers we not only need to help people to focus on and hear these better stories, we need also to work against injustice and violence so that people can see themselves reflected in these better stories.

NOTE

1. All biblical citations are taken from the New Revised Standard Version.

REFERENCES

Barré, Michael L. "Fasting in Isaiah 58:1–12: A Reexamination." *Biblical Theology Bulletin* 15 (1985): 94–97.

Beker, J. Christiaan. *Paul the Apostle: The Triumph of God in Life and Thought.* Philadelphia: Fortress Press, 1984.

Betz, Hans Dieter. "The Sermon on the Mount." *Hermeneia.* Minneapolis: Fortress Press, 1995.

Brettler, Marc. "Images of YHWH the Warrior in the Psalms. " *Semeia* 61 (1993): 135–65.

Bright, John. *Jeremiah.* Anchor Bible 21. Garden City, N. Y. : Doubleday, 1965.

Brown, Raymond. *The Gospel According to John (i–xii).* Anchor Bible 20. Garden City, N. Y. : Doubleday, 1966.

Crossan, John Dominic. *The Historical Jesus: The Life of a Mediterranean Jewish Peasant.* New York: HarperCollins, 1991.

Di Lella, Alexander A., and Patrick W. Skehan. *The Wisdom of Ben Sira.* Anchor Bible 39. Garden City, N. Y. : Doubleday, 1987.

Fitzmyer, Joseph A. "Introduction to the New Testament Epistles." *The New Jerome Biblical Commentary.* Englewood Cliffs, N. J. : Prentice Hall, 1990.

Fretheim, Terence E. "The Reclamation of Creation. Redemption and Law in Exodus." *Interpretation* 45 (1991): 354–65.

_____. "'Because the Whole Earth is Mine' Theme and Narrative in Exodus." *Interpretation* 50 (1996): 229–39.

Furnish, Victor Paul. "War and Peace in the New Testament." *Interpretation* 38 (1984): 363–79.

Girard, René. *Violence and the Sacred*. Baltimore: Johns Hopkins, 1979.

_____. *The Scapegoat*. Baltimore: Johns Hopkins, 1986.

Hamerton-Kelly, Robert. "A Girardian Interpretation of Paul's Rivalry, Mimesis and Victimage in the Corinthian Correspondence." *Semeia* 33 (1985): 65–81.

Hanson, Paul D. "War and Peace in the Hebrew Bible." *Interpretation* 38 (1984): 341–62.

Harrington, Wilfrid J. "Revelation." *Sacra Pagina* 16. Collegeville, Minn.: The Liturgical Press, 1993.

Hays, Richard B. *The Moral Vision of the New Testament: A Contemporary Introduction to New Testament Ethics*. New York: HarperCollins, 1996.

Hobbs, T. R. "A Time For War: A Study of Warfare in the Old Testament." *Old Testament Studies* 3. Wilmington, Del.: Michael Glazier, 1989.

Holladay, William L. Jeremiah 1: *A Commentary on the Book of the Prophet Jeremiah, Chapters 1–25. Hermeneia*. Philadelphia: Fortress Press, 1986.

Hoppe, L. J. "Isaiah 58:1–12, Fasting and Idolatry." *Biblical Theology Bulletin* 13 (1983): 44–47.

Keefe, Alice A. "Rapes of Women/Wars of Men." *Semeia* 61 (1993): 79–98.

Kenner, Hugh. *The Pound Era*. Berkeley and Los Angeles: University of California Press, 1971.

Lohfink, N. "Herem." *Theological Dictionary of the Old Testament*. V. 180–99. Grand Rapids: Eerdmans, 1986.

McKenzie, John L. *Second Isaiah*. Anchor Bible 20. Garden City, N.Y. : Doubleday, 1968.

Miller, Patrick D. "God the Warrior: A Problem in Biblical Interpretation and Apologetics." *Interpretation* 19 (1965): 39–46.

Niditch, Susan. "War, Women, and Defilement in Numbers 31." *Semeia* 61 (1993): 39–57.

O'Day, Gail R. "The Gospel of John: Introduction, Commentary, and Reflections." Volume IX. *The New Interpreter's Bible*. Nashville: Abingdon Press, 1995.

Pannenberg, Wolfhart. *Systematic Theology*. Volume 2. Grand Rapids: Eerdmans, 1994.

Schnackenburg, Rudolf. *The Gospel According to St. John*. New York: Herder, 1968.

Stuhlmueller, Carroll. "Deutero-Isaiah and Trito-Isaiah." *The New Jerome Biblical Commentary*. Englewood Cliffs, N.J.: Prentice Hall, 1990.

Ulrich, Eugene C., and William G. Thompson. "The Tradition as a Resource in Theological Reflection—Scripture and the Minister." *Method in Ministry: Theological Reflection and Christian Ministry.* New York: The Seabury Press, 1980.

Von Rad, Gerhard. *Holy War in Ancient Israel.* Grand Rapids: Eerdmans, 1991.

Weinfeld, Moshe. *Social Justice in Ancient Israel and in the Ancient Near East.* Minneapolis: Fortress Press, 1995.

Westermann, Claus. *Genesis 1—11.* Minneapolis: Augsburg Press, 1984.

Whitehead, James D., and Evelyn Eaton Whitehead, eds. *Method in Ministry. Theological Reflection and Christian Ministry.* Kansas City: Sheed & Ward, 1995.

Whybray, Roger Norman. *Isaiah 40—66.* New Century Bible Commentary. Grand Rapids: Eerdmans, 1981.

Williams, James G. "The Innocent Victim: René Girard on Violence, Sacrifice, and the Sacred." *Religious Studies Review* 14 (1988): 320–26.

_____. *The Bible, Violence, and the Sacred: Liberation from the Myth of Sanctioned Violence.* San Francisco: HarperCollins, 1991.

Human Dignity, Human Rights, and Ecology: Christian, Buddhist, and Native American Perspectives

James S. Dalton

I. THE ROOTS OF HUMAN DIGNITY

Underlying the issue of the meaning of human dignity at the end of the twentieth century is the question of how such dignity can be derived. In other words, why should human beings have importance and what accounts for this importance? This chapter is intended to address, in a preliminary fashion, such questions in the context of a crosscultural dialogue. By looking at the roots of human dignity from the perspective of Christian, Buddhist, and Native American traditions and examining the consequences of these perspectives for human dignity, it might be possible to broaden the discussion of such critical issues as human rights and ecology.

Such a discussion cannot do justice to the complexity of Western or non-Western traditions and their contributions to the study of human dignity and what threatens this dignity. Any religious tradition exhibits a variety of positions on issues of human dignity, human rights, and the environment. Ann Elizabeth Mayer's observations on religion and human rights in Islam can serve to illustrate a point that applies to all of the traditions under consideration in this chapter.

> ...one should not speak of "Islam" and human rights as if Islam were a monolith or as if there existed one settled Islamic human rights philosophy that caused all Muslims to look at rights in a particular way. The precepts of Islam, like those of Christianity, Hinduism, Judaism, and other major religions possessed of long and complex traditions, are susceptible to interpretations that can and do create conflicts

between religious doctrine and human rights norms or that
reconcile the two. In reality, one cannot predict the position
that a person will take on a human rights problem simply on
the basis of the person's religious affiliation—and this is as
true of Muslims as of members of other faiths. (Mayer,
1995, *xi*)

One must recognize that Christian conceptions of human dignity, ecology, and human rights are also complex both in their historical and contemporary manifestations. As will be seen later, this must be said of Buddhist and Native American views as well. The present chapter can only point to some of the more dominant trends within these traditions. More scholarly studies will have to identify and examine the nuances of such Christian, Buddhist, and Native American concepts.

The difficulties of examining notions that historically arose within the Christian tradition must not deter us from looking at these notions from other than Western points of reference. As a matter of fact, such an examination is crucial for these Western-derived concepts. Only within the context of a truly crosscultural dialogue will ideas of human dignity be truly and finally meaningful. It is assumed that such a dialogue is possible between cultural and religious traditions despite the position of cultural relativists who believe that such traditions can only be understood in their own terms and cannot be compared one to another. Thus they "tend to endorse the idea that all values and principles are culturebound and that there are no universals" (Mayer, 1995, 9). "Religious traditions," as Charles Strain points out, speaking of human rights, "provide an important corrective to the Western liberal interpretation of human rights by situating rights within a larger understanding of the common good and of ultimate purpose" (Strain, 1995, 3). It is one of the implicit understandings of this paper that a crosscultural dialogue on human rights and the environment has become an essential requirement at the end of the twentieth and the beginning of the twenty-first centuries. As a matter of fact, it is assumed that such a dialogue represents a pastoral imperative for Catholics (as well as for many other Christians), as will be argued in the conclusion of this chapter.

The central argument of this discussion is that human dignity, attested to by Christians, Buddhists, and Native Americans, is not held by all of them for the same reasons. In the Western tradition human dignity is rooted in the creative act of God. For Buddhists and traditional Native Americans, on the other hand, it is the embeddedness of human beings in the wider context of reality that grounds human dignity. In other words, human beings are inextricably interrelated with all other beings and do not have a "privileged" place among them. The consequences of these differing perspectives will become apparent as this discussion continues.

II. THE WESTERN TRADITION, HUMAN RIGHTS, AND ECOLOGY

A. Biblical and Christian Roots

> Then God said, "Let us make humankind in our image, according to our likeness; and let them have dominion over the fish of the sea, and over the birds of the air, and over the cattle, and over all the wild animals of the earth, and over every creeping thing that creeps upon the earth."
>
> So God created humankind in his image, in the image of God he created them: male and female he created them. God blessed them, and God said to them, "Be fruitful and multiply, and fill the earth and subdue it; and have dominion over the fish of the sea and over the birds of the air and over every living thing that moves upon the earth." God said, "See, I have given you every plant yielding seed that is upon the face of all the earth, and every tree with seed in its fruit; you shall have them for food. And to every beast of the earth, and to every bird of the air, and to everything that creeps on the earth, everything that has the breath of life, I have given every green plant for food." And it was so. (Gn 1:26–30)[1]

Thus begins, in the charter document of the Christian tradition, the history of human dignity and its relationship to the world of "nature." The history of this text and its interpretations have been varied and complex as is illustrated in the work of Dianne Bergant (Bergant, 1985; Bergant, 1991). However, according to the dominant interpretation, humankind is *created* in the image of God (Scullion, 1998). Further, human beings are intended to *dominate* the natural world around them.

Reinforcing this latter emphasis, Genesis goes on to define the relationship of humankind and animals: "So out of the ground the Lord God formed every animal of the field and every bird of the air, and brought them to the man to see what he would call them; and whatever the man called every living creature, that was its name" (Gn 2:19–20). In the ancient world the process of naming is more that simply one of designation. To name is to give reality. In other words, Adam, by naming the animals gives them their proper meaning in the world. The reality of animals is *defined* by humans.

In the Western Christian tradition the notion that human reality is created in the image of God and restored in Jesus Christ is the foundation for further speculation on the dignity of the human person. This is then linked with domination over the natural world. The rights and privileges that accrue to human reality take precedence over those of animals, plants, and inanimate reality. All of nature finds its culmination and meaning in human reality created by God and redeemed in Jesus Christ. So powerful is this linkage of the human and natural orders that all of nature is seen to have fallen in the fall of Adam and Eve. Only in Jesus Christ is nature restored to its fullest meaning and purpose as manifesting the glory of God and contributing to the realization of human meaning and salvation.

Medieval Christianity further elaborated on these realities in what has come to be called "the Great Chain of Being." Human beings resided at its center with angels above and animals, plants and inanimate nature below. The importance of human reality was emphasized not only in its role as the "crown of creation" but also in its control of the orders of being below it. Human dignity, from the Christian perspective, came from its having been created in the "image of God." At the same time human control of nature was implicit in its position in the Great Chain of Being and explicit in the biblical texts of Genesis quoted above. Thus human dignity and ecology are linked in the Western Christian perspective.

B. The Enlightenment: Human Dignity and Human Rights

The Renaissance, and especially the Enlightenment of the seventeenth and eighteenth centuries, represented a fundamental turning point in the foundations of Western conceptions of human rights. Earlier doctrines of human "duties" gave way to the conviction that human "rights" should be central in political theory and a preoccupation of political philosophy. The bases for modern human rights theory was laid at that time (Mayer, 1995, 37).

Christianity had previously emphasized the salvation of the individual within the context of the salvation of the community (the church). With the Renaissance, Reformation, and Enlightenment (fifteenth to eighteenth centuries), the individual became more central in religious as well as political thinking. The dignity of the human person now became identified with the dignity of the individual "grounded in a new view of the nature of man, and the relationship of each individual to others and to society" (Pollis, 1979, 2). Human beings were now understood to be autonomous and in possession of certain inalienable "rights." Rooted in the political philosophies of Aristotle and Cicero and expressed in seventeenth-century thinkers such as Sir Edward Coke, Thomas Hooker, John Milton, John Locke, and Jean Jacques Rousseau, belief grew "that there are universal standards and values that are discernible by rational beings and that these are inherent to the human condition" (Powers, 1995, 5). These ideas profoundly influenced such documents as the English Petition of Rights (1627), the Habeas Corpus Act (1679), the American Declaration of Independence (1776), the US Constitution (1787), and the Declaration of the Rights of Man and Citizen (1789) during the French Revolution (Pollis, 1979, 2).

C. Human Rights and Ecology in the Twentieth Century

The debate over human rights has become one of the most pervasive themes of the late twentieth century in the West as well as in the wider international community. The touchstone for the vast literature about human rights has been The Universal Declaration of Human Rights, which was passed by the United Nations General Assembly on December 10, 1948 (United Nations).

Whereas recognition of the inherent dignity and of the equal and inalienable rights of all members of the human family is the foundation of freedom, justice and peace in the world...

Proclaims
THIS UNIVERSAL DECLARATION OF HUMAN
RIGHTS as a common standard of achievement for all
peoples and all nations…. (United Nations, 1)

Attacks on the United Nations *Declaration* have come not only from countries with less than admirable human rights records (as an attack on their national sovereignty) but also from communitarians (who object to its "individualistic" emphasis) and cultural relativists (who identify the assumptions of human rights theory as being specifically Western and, therefore, not applicable to other cultures). The communitarian and cultural relativist arguments raise significant issues relating to the notion of human rights. The UN *Declaration* enumerates various violations of human rights that could also be considered threats to human dignity. These rights include life, liberty, the security of person (Article 3), freedom from torture (Article 5), equal protection before the law (Articles 6–11), privacy (Article 12), freedom of movement (Articles 13–15), property (Article 17), thought, conscience and religion (Articles 18–19), political rights (Articles 20–21), economic rights (Articles 23–25), education (Article 26), and cultural life (Article 27). Needless to say, these rights and their applicability to various national and cultural situations has been hotly and extensively debated.

A second major crisis of the twentieth century concerns the environment of the planet earth. The ecological movement has raised anew the threat to human dignity, even to human survival itself, that is posed by the degradation of the environment. Elements as diverse as the question of global warming, the survival of the great rain forests with their biodiversity, and the appropriate use of the raw materials of the earth have been a matter of public discussion and debate. Many scholars and commentators have recognized the religious dimensions of this crisis as well. Christians themselves have raised questions about the human "domination" of nature rooted in the Christian, Jewish, and Islamic traditions. There seems to be a growing recognition that

…atheists and Christians alike have tended to define Western civilization as effective "exploitation of the earth by man" and "protection against the forces of nature." To be civilized is to be free of nature, to rise above and transcend nature, to shield oneself from nature and exploit it (Vecsey, 1980, 36).

III. BUDDHISM, INTERDEPENDENCE, ECOLOGY, AND HUMAN RIGHTS

He conquers and is not conquered,
none in the world enters what he conquers,
he is the Buddha, the enlightened one,
infinitely aware, leader of himself,
impossible to describe in the languages of men.
No desires like nets trap him,
no passions like poison affect him.
He is the Buddha, the enlightened one,
infinitely aware, leader of himself,
impossible to describe in the languages of men.
Even the gods imitate wise men,
the enlightened, the dignified, the meditating, the free.
Hard it is to get born human,
hard it is to live like a human;
hard it is to listen to Dhamma,
hard to achieve the state of enlightenment. (Lal, 1967, 101)

A. Human Reality in the Buddhist Tradition

A radically different perspective on human reality and human dignity is represented by the Buddhist religious tradition. Buddhism places little or no importance on the existence of a transcendent God. Buddhism denies the reality of the human self or any unchanging or enduring reality of any sort underlying beings. Finally, Buddhism is a religion composed of varying traditions such as the Theravada (the oldest, which is found in Sri Lanka and Southeast Asia), Mahayana (in East Asia), and Vajrayana (in Tibet). Although these traditions have varying ideas about the nature and meaning of Buddhahood and the exact path to enlightenment, most scholars would argue that they are expressions of a single tradition that shares the fundamental starting points of the Buddha: the *Dharma* (the teachings of the Buddha and its sacred, saving reality) and the *Sangha* (the Buddhist community, especially the monastic community).

Buddhism represents one of the most profound religious understandings of human reality, its nature and goals, and the path to salvation that exists in human culture. So powerful is this Buddhist perspective that many Westerners have been attracted to it, either by becoming practicing Buddhists or by integrating Buddhism into their own religious traditions. This integration of Buddhist practice into the lives of non-Buddhists indicates a religious vision that could make significant contributions to Western notions of human dignity, ecology, and human rights.

Buddhism does not recognize a transcendent creator God and, where belief in God or gods prevails, it sees them as largely irrelevant to the pursuit of salvation or, in Buddhist terms, final enlightenment.

> In contrast [to Christianity], Buddhism does not talk about the One absolute God who is essentially transcendent to human beings. Instead, it teaches the *Dharma,* which is *pratitya-samutpada,* the law of "dependent co-origination" or conditional co-production. This teaching emphasizes that everything *in* and *beyond* the universe is interdependent, co-arising, and co-ceasing (not only temporarily but also logically): nothing exists independently or can be said to be self-existing. Accordingly, in Buddhism everything without exception is relative, relational, nonsubstantial, and changeable. (Abe, 1986, 194)

Such a religious view has enormous consequences for human life and aspirations, as Masao Abe (a Zen master conversant with Western religion and philosophy) further observes:

> When the divine, God or Buddha, is believed to be self-affirmative, self-existing, enduring, and substantial, the divine becomes authoritative, commanding, and intolerant. On the contrary, when the divine, God or Buddha, is believed to be self-negating, relational, and nonsubstantial, the divine becomes compassionate, all-loving, and tolerant. (Abe, 1986, 210)

In order to understand Buddhist attitudes toward ecology and human rights, it is necessary to unpack the Buddhist anthropology, which Abe outlined above. In the first place, Buddhism recognizes three characteristics of existence: impermanence *(anitya),* suffering *(dukkha),* and non-self *(anatman).* Impermanence is the quality of existence that ensures that *all beings will change and pass away.*

What is born will die,

What has been gathered will be dispersed,
What has been accumulated will be exhausted,
What has been built up will collapse,
What has been high will be brought low. (Sogyal, 1994, 26)

Suffering *(dukkha)* is the quality of existence that served as the starting point of the Buddha's path to enlightenment. Inherent in the fabric of life, *dukkha* is equivalent to the general "unsatisfactoriness" of life. The Buddha referred, in his first sermon, to birth, aging, sickness, death, sorrow, lamentation, pain, grief, despair, association with the disliked, separation from the liked, and not getting what one wants as *dukkha* (Harvey, 1990, 47–48). This is called the First Noble Truth of Buddhism. The Second Noble Truth is that the cause of *dukkha* is craving or desire *(tanha)*. The Third Noble Truth is that there is a condition of the overcoming of desire, which is called *Nirvana*. The Fourth Noble Truth is the path to *Nirvana,* the Noble Eightfold Path or the Middle Way of Buddhism.

The third quality of existence is non-self *(anatman)*.

> Buddhist analysis of the nature of the person centers on the realization that what appears to be an individual is, in fact, an ever-changing combination of five constituent factors or building blocks *(shandha;* Pali, *khanda)*: the physical body *(rupa),* physical sensation *(vedana),* sense perception *(samjna, sanna)* habitual tendencies *(samskara, samkhara),* and consciousness *(vijnana, vinnana).* (Mahoney, 1988, 442)

This belief is a consequence of the Buddhist conviction that there is no underlying, permanent reality to any being since all beings are impermanent. The individual soul, as Christians conceive of it, which endures even beyond death, does not exist for Buddhists. According to G. P. Malalasekera, "An individual is a being, that is, something that is, but, in the Buddha's teaching, the individual's being is, in fact, a *becoming,* a coming-to-be, something that happens, that is, an event, a process" (Malalasekera, 1964, 146).

If there are no permanent realities that underlie existence, then how do Buddhists account for human beings and the universe they inhabit? The answer to this question and the fundamental principle that enables a Buddhist ecology and a Buddhist understanding of human rights (although modified from Western conceptions) is called dependent co-origination *(pratitya-samutpada)*. This difficult and complex notion might be summarized in the statement that all beings are interdependent and relational.

It means that, in any life-process, the arising of an experiential event is a total, relational affair. A particular event does not arise in a vacuum, nor does it result by the imposition of external forces or elements. It is a unique arisal that is vitally dependent on or related to all the elements present within the surroundings. Thus, in the process there is nothing that is fragmentary or has any gaps, since it relates with the complete fullness of all the elements present. Each relationship is full insofar as the process is concerned. This means that relational origination is a most concrete way in which life-process goes on. (Inada, 1982, 70)

The consequences of this Buddhist principle for ecology and human rights will be examined below.

One major implication of dependent co-origination that is drawn out by the Mahayana tradition of Buddhism is the notion of compassion *(karuna)* realized most fully in the *Bodhisattva,* who is a being who refuses to complete the process of enlightenment until all beings are enlightened. Compassion "means passion for all in an ontologically extensive sense. It covers the realm of all sentient beings, inclusive of nonsentients, for the doors of perception to total reality are always open" (Inada, 1990, 8). The *Bodhisattva* is perpetually at the service of all beings due to great compassion.

B. Buddhism and Ecology: The Interdependence of Being

Buddhists do not separate human reality from the reality of nature, although the human state is the best platform for the attainment of enlightenment. The principles of non-self and dependent co-origination lead, according to Masao Abe, in another direction.

The self and nature are different from one another on the relative level, but on the absolute level they are equal and interfuse with one another because of the lack of any fixed, substantial selfhood. Consequently, nature is not merely a resource for the human self; it is grasped in sympathetic relationship with the self. (Abe, 1986, 205)

Human beings, for Abe, "are grasped as a part of all sentient beings or even as a part of all beings, sentient and nonsentient, because both human and nonhuman beings are equally subject to transiency or impermanency" (Abe, 1986, 202). And further, "Under the commandment 'Not to destroy any life,' the rights of animals and plants are as equally recognized as are human rights. Not only is nature subordinate to human beings, but human beings are also subordinate to nature" (Abe, 1986, 205).

In summary, Buddhist understandings of the relationship of human reality and nature is holistic and cosmological. Since all reality is perceived by us as relational and interdependent, a strict separation of human reality and natural reality is not possible, as it is for Christianity. As Abe pointed out above, humans are also subordinate to nature as nature is subordinate to humans. When one combines this with the Mahayana notion of compassion *(karuna),* the human/natural relationship is one of caring and mutuality. Buddhism, then, is ecological in its core understanding of the very nature of reality. Buddhist contributions to a dialogue on the environment, therefore, are significant and suggestive. Unfortunately, to this point, these contributions have not become important for the contemporary ecological discussion.

C. Buddhism and Human Rights

Buddhist ecological principles can be extended to the contemporary discussion of human dignity and human rights. This is evidently the case in the view of the Dalai Lama who gave a major address to the United Nations World Conference on Human Rights on June 15, 1993, in Vienna, Austria. The title of his address was "Human Rights and Universal Responsibility." According to His Holiness,

No matter what country or continent we come from we are all basically the same human beings. We have the common human needs and concerns. We all seek happiness and try to avoid suffering regardless of our race, religion, sex or political

status. Human beings, indeed all sentient beings, have the right
to pursue happiness and live in peace and in freedom.... The
key to creating a better and more peaceful world is the development of love and compassion for others.... When I traveled
to Europe for the first time in 1973, I talked about the increasing interdependence of the world and the need to develop a
sense of universal responsibility. (Dalai Lama, 1–2)

The Dalai Lama further endorses the *Universal Declaration of Human
Rights* and rejects the positions of Asian nations (especially China) who
reject the *Declaration*. He further rejects the argument from cultural rel-
ativism that maintains the inapplicability of these principles to Asian
cultures. As a Buddhist, he argues even further, "Human rights, environmental protection and great social and economic equality, are all interrelated" (Dalai Lama, 3). The position of the Dalai Lama is, of course,
rooted in the Buddhist notions of non-self, dependent co-origination,
and compassion.

It is important to remember, however, that, for Buddhists, the term
"human rights" remains somewhat problematic. Properly speaking, *all*
beings share in these rights. Whereas, in the Western view, rights accrue
primarily to individual human beings, "the Buddhist understands human
experience as a totally open phenomenon, that persons should always be
wide open in the living process" (Inada, 1990, 6–7). Buddhism, then, is
uncomfortable with Western individualism not only because of its own
doctrine of non-self, but also because individualism violates the basic
interrelatedness of all beings.

Western civilization is often criticized by Buddhists as being
excessively individualistic. "Human rights" may be criticized
on similar grounds. The notion of inalienable rights, somehow inherent in the individual, who then is encouraged to
demand recognition, not only partakes of that individualism,
but intensifies it, perhaps strengthening the very "I" which
Buddhism advises us to weaken. (Evans, 1995, 2)

Santipala Stephen Evans further argues for a Buddhist conception of
human rights rooted in a Buddhist anthropology (Evans, 1995, 1–13).
Such an anthropology would see rights as pertaining to all beings in
their relatedness to all other beings.

D. Buddhism and Catholic Social Teaching: A Proposal

Charles R. Strain, Professor of Religious Studies at DePaul University, has proposed a dialogue between Roman Catholics and Buddhists in a paper entitled "Socially Engaged Buddhism's Contribution to the Transformation of Catholic Social Teachings on Human Rights." He argues that

> religious traditions advocating human rights provide an important corrective to Western liberal interpretations of human rights by situating rights within a larger understanding of the common good and of ultimate purpose. Secondly, religious traditions by forging alliances across religious and cultural divides using such "bridge concepts" as human rights are the key to meeting the challenges of cultural relativists. (Strain, 1995, 1)

Strain believes that special attention should be paid to the Buddhist notion of dependent co-origination (he calls it "dependent co-arising") which could "lead Catholic thinkers and activists to reconsider and reformulate a series of central principles underlying Catholic social teachings on human rights" (Strain, 1995, 1). Buddhist concerns with the anthropocentric quality of Western conceptions of human rights with their implicit "entitlement" status and their tendency to become adversarial (and thus to ignore consensual models of society), must be addressed (Strain, 1995, 8). However, as he points out,

> Those of us who root ourselves in Catholic social teachings find common ground with engaged Buddhists in a fundamental distrust of the individualistic assumptions underlying the Western, liberal tradition which spawned the struggle for human rights. (Strain, 1995, 9)

Further, he suggests that the Catholic principle of subsidiarity might be fruitfully linked to Thich Nhat Hanh's "Order of Interbeing" (a Vietnamese Buddhist proposal for the insertion of activists between warring ideologies, factions, and oppositional systems) (Strain, 1995, 11–13). Engaged Buddhism, he points out, is seeking the "Middle Way" (a term often used by Buddhists to describe the Buddhist religion) between

Western social models of greed and self-indulgence and totalitarian models of state socialism (Strain, 1995, 9).

Finally, Strain proposes a linkage between Catholic Trinitarian theology and Buddhist dependent co-arising. "Conceiving God's trinitarian presence in the world in light of the dependent coarising's qualities of mutuality, holism and emptiness might lead to a fluid, relational sense of cosmic cocreation (Strain, 1995, 13).

Strain's proposal is offered as one possibility among many for a Buddhist-Christian dialogue on human rights. Buddhist ecological and holistic understandings in Theravada, Mahayana, and Vajrayana traditions might also be fruitful. It should be remembered that the Dalai Lama is the head of one of the most important schools of Tibetan (Vajrayana) Buddhism. His tireless pursuit of human rights from his own Buddhist perspective offers fresh and important insights into the questions of human dignity that should not be left unexplored.

Buddhist-Christian dialogues, up to the present time, have tended to focus on meditation and spiritual experience. Without denigrating this important religious dialogue, it might be suggested that a further dialogue on issues such as human dignity and the environment might now be fruitfully pursued. Initiatives, such as that of the *Journal of Buddhist Ethics* online conference on Buddhism and human rights are promising beginnings.

IV. NATIVE AMERICAN RELIGIONS AND ECOLOGY

You ask me to plough the ground! Shall I take a knife and tear my mother's bosom? Then when I die she will not take me to her bosom to rest.

You ask me to cut grass and make hay and sell it, and be rich like white men, but how dare I cut off my mother's hair. (Gill, 1983, 157)

The question of human dignity is not only linked to that of human rights, it is also linked to the environment in which human beings are embedded. Nowhere is this more visible than in the experience of the native peoples of the world. The native experience has often been used as the model for ecological consciousness, a notion which, as we shall see, is often more romantic than it is true to the cultures that are described. On the other hand, the experience of native peoples, specifically Native Americans, can present us with alternative ways of thinking about the relationship of human reality to the reality of nature. Before these ways can be explored, however, some cautions are in order.

A. Cautions: Diversity and Stereotypes

Despite general terms such as "Native American" or "Indian" we are not dealing with a unified cultural tradition but rather with a plurality of differing cultures. These cultures are spread across an entire continent inhabiting widely differing environments and landscapes. Native experiences of their environments, therefore, differ one from another and their ways of encoding these experiences in their cultures also differ.

> Given aboriginal peoples' long habitation of Turtle Island (the name for North America used by many aboriginal peoples), and respecting the great diversity of their societies, it is extremely hazardous to generalize about aboriginal attitudes to the land and the environment. Furthermore, as is true of European and other traditions, aboriginal concepts of land tenure and use are intricately and precisely specific to particular societies and to the circumstances in which those societies found themselves. The concepts and laws of aboriginal land use evolved in response to changes in aboriginal peoples' environmental and economic circumstances, and they continue to evolve today. (Abele, 1994, 598)

Ake Hultkrantz, an eminent scholar of Native American religions, argues that "every experience of nature varies according to the 'culture type'" of Native traditions (Hultkrantz, 1981, 120) and that "the Indian veneration of nature is specific, not general" (Hultkrantz, 1981, 122). Different conceptions and uses of nature exist among, for example, hunting peoples and agricultural peoples in the Americas (Hultkrantz, 1981, 120–22). Great caution must be used when generalizing about the Native American relationship to the environment in light of the diversity of cultures and landscapes that exist.

A second caution is necessary in light of the historical development of Native American peoples, especially under the impact of European contact. Native peoples, in the first place, are not ahistorical. They exist, and have always existed, in changing historical and environmental situations both prior to and after contact with Europeans. There is not, nor has there ever been, a "state of nature" inhabited by unchanging native peoples either "savage" or "noble"! Thus there cannot be an eternal and enduring Native American ecology.

The third caution concerns the images or stereotypes of Native Americans that have grown up since Columbus's journey to the New World in 1492. The first image is that of the "noble savage" which sees Native Americans "as nature folk whose nobility, freedom, and spontaneity derive from their close association with the land" (Vecsey, 1980, 3). This image of the Native American has more to do with European's dissatisfaction with their own societies and, more recently, with their guilt over environmental exploitation than it does with Native American cultures or religions.

The second stereotype of Native Americans might be referred to as the "savage" or "wild" Indian who, as part of wild and savage "nature," "are not to be emulated, as in the tradition that Rousseau epitomized. Rather, their way of life is something to be overcome, repressed, and destroyed" (Vecsey, 1980, 3). The tragic consequences of this latter image are well documented in the history of Native Americans in the nineteenth and twentieth centuries. The implication of this image for the environment is that nature, which is wild and disorderly, needs to be tamed, exploited, and controlled. The human order and the natural order are definitively separated.

B. Human Reality and Human Dignity in Native America

Despite the diversity of Native American traditions some common themes can be found, especially with regard to nature and the environment. Although creation stories concerning the appearance of human beings range from those that attribute that creation to a culture hero such as Raven (on the Northeast Coast), Rabbit (in the Southeast) and Old Man (on the Plains), emergence from under the earth (Navajo, Pueblo, and Apache), or earth-divers (Winnebago, Zuni), they all seem to emphasize the embeddedness of human beings in the natural world and the necessity of maintaining harmonious relationships between various kinds of beings. The Navajo emergence myth, for instance, "emphasizes a search for moral responsibility, seeking a state of being in which humans, plants, animals, sun, and moon exist in a stabilized, moral, and harmonious relationship" (Morrison, 1994, 636). Earth-diver myths "are similar in that they teach that all persons, human and otherwise, must share power and responsibility" (Morrison, 1994, 637). Vine Deloria, Jr., in an important statement of Native American religious thought (*God Is Red: A Native View of Religion,* Fulcrum, 1994) contrasts Christian and Native approaches to creation:

> ...a very major distinction that can be made between the two types of thinking concerns the idea of creation. Christianity has traditionally appeared to place its major emphasis on creation as a specific event, while the Indian tribal religions could be said to consider creation as an ecosystem present in a definable place....Both religions can be said to agree on the role and activity of a creator....Tribal religions appear to be thereafter confronted with the question of the interrelationship of all things. (Deloria, 1994, 78)

The human order, then, is embedded in and interrelated with the natural order. Humans are capable of causing disturbances in this order which bring about disorder and destruction. The maintenance of harmony is essential to guarantee the proper functioning of the world of humans, animals, plants, and spirits. "Mother Earth reminds her people that her well being depends on responsible human action" (Morrison, 1994, 647). According to Sam Gill, Navajo religion serves such a purpose.

> The world was created in perfect beauty, but perfect beauty means a static order; since life is a dynamic process requiring movement, it risks destroying this beauty; so as disorder arises and life is threatened, one must be able to reconstitute order and beauty in the world; and this is done by ceremonial means, which recreate the pattern of perfect beauty. (Gill, 1982, 34)

Ordinary reality and cosmic reality symbolically correspond to each other (Gill, 1982, 87).

Human dignity, then, is inseparable from the cosmic order of being. For Native American traditions it simply does not make sense to talk about the importance of human reality (although this importance is certainly affirmed) without relationship to the beings, both spiritual and material, that Europeans have called "natural" or "supernatural."

> Their primary world view is that the human and non-human worlds are not separated by distinct boundaries. Distinctions between species, or between animate and inanimate forms, do not have the same significance as in non-Indian U.S. society. Within the Indian system, the natural world contains spiritual powers in the forms of animals, birds, fish, plants, the sun, the moon, and within natural phenomena such as rain and thunder. Human beings are only one part of a complex natural world and are not superior to the other parts. In order to function with the world, these powers must be reckoned with, primarily through rituals, which take the form of specific religious ceremonies but are also a part of the daily activities necessary for life. (Crowe, 1994, 593)

Although Native Americans regard nature as the ultimate source of their existence, they also recognize that their relationship with other orders of reality are often dissonant. In addition to regarding nature with reverence and piety, they also feared it since, for their survival (physically, culturally, and religiously), they were also were forced to exploit it in various ways (hunting, planting, and so forth). Stephen Vecsey even speculates that their attitude involved a sense of guilt. Hunters apologized to their game, and thanked them in order that they might kill them in the future.

> To say that Indians existed in harmony with nature is a half-truth. Indians were both a part of nature and apart from nature in their own world view. They utilized the environment extensively, realized the differences between human and nonhuman persons, and felt guilt for their exploitation of nature's live-giving life. (Vecsey, 1980, 23)

Although some Native Americans have questioned the appropriateness of this notion of "environmental guilt" (Vecsey, 1980, 181, note 83), it is clear that human beings are in an ambivalent relationship to other beings and powers in the cosmos. The stereotype of the Native American as a "natural environmentalist" in constant harmony with nature is an extension of the "noble savage" image of the eighteenth century and does not adequately represent the reality of this complex relationship. In the Native American religious perspective,

> the world is composed of persons, not things; some persons, including some human beings, are powerful; some are not; some persons act in caring, respectful, and nurturing ways; many do not. In brief, all people have responsibilities toward others, whether or not they act accordingly. (Morrison, 1994, 648)

Vine Deloria, a contemporary Native American "theologian," contrasts the Christian view of nature as "fallen" in the sin of Adam and Eve with the Native American belief in the goodness of nature.

> For many Indian tribal religions the whole of creation was good, and because the creation event did not include a "fall," the meaning of creation was that all parts of it functioned together to sustain it. Young Chief, a Cayuse, refused to sign the Treaty of Walla Walla because he felt the rest of the creation was not represented in the transaction. (Deloria, 1994, 81)

C. Native American Ecology in the Twentieth Century

Despite the belief of some non-Native Americans in the twentieth century, Native Americans did not correspond to the image of them as "vanishing Americans." Quite the contrary, there has been a significant revival of traditional Native American religious and cultural ways, even among those who are Christians (see Gill, 1982, 140–73). However, the tragic history of Native Americans over the last century and a half (especially the history of their removal from their traditional lands) damaged Native religious and cultural traditions.

> Displacement hurt Indians on all levels of environmental relation. It took them away from the herbs, plants, hunting

grounds, and other places which they knew in such detail. It made Indian subsistence extremely precarious because upon removal an Indian group would have to learn a new territory, become familiar with it in pragmatic ways in order to exploit it efficiently. This took time. Removal also meant taking Indians from places charged with meaning and emotion. Indians were dislocated from sacred space, where they had once emerged from their mother earth, where revelations occurred, where their ancestors were buried, where the powers of a living earth nurtured them. (Vecsey, 1980, 26)

It would seem that the development of principles of human dignity as well as principles of sound ecology would necessitate addressing this situation in the Americas as well as in the rest of the world where native peoples have suffered similar fates. As Lawrence Sullivan has stated, "[T]he spiritual universes of the indigenous peoples of the Americas remain to this day largely unexplored by outsiders" (Sullivan, 1988, 8). This exploration is not only necessary for the well-being of Native Americans, it is crucial for the survival and dignity of *all* Americans.

Reports of the New World brim with contradictions because, deep in the European religious imagination—the generative foundation of its culture—the experience of "discovery," the encounter of contrasting modes of cultural being, was one of disturbing ambivalence. Modernity still shapes its self-conceptions around the responses to this religious situation. (Sullivan, 1988, 7)

In other words, a dialogue with Native Americans concerning the nature and dignity of the human person and the relationship of human beings to their cosmic setting is necessary for the religious self-understanding of the Christian tradition in the twenty-first century. Chief John Snow underlines this necessity in his statement of the contemporary Native American view of nature.

We believe that the Creator made everything beautiful in his time. We believe that we must be good stewards of the Creator and not destroy nor mar His works of creation. We look upon stewardship not only in terms of money and the profit of a hundredfold, but in those of respect for the beauty of the land and of life in harmony with the succession of the seasons, so that the voices of all living things can be heard and continue to live and dwell among us. If an area is destroyed, marred, or polluted, my people say, the spirits will leave the area. If pollution continues not only animals, birds, and plant life will disappear, but the spirits will also leave. This is one of the greatest concerns of Indian people. (quoted in Hultkrantz, 1981, 127)

V. CROSSCULTURAL DIALOGUE: THE PASTORAL DIMENSION

As indicated above, at the end of the twentieth century, Christians can no longer ignore the perspectives and religious traditions of other cultures. The Catholic Church recognized this in its "Declaration on the Relation of the Church to Non-Christian Religions" *(Nostra Aetate)* of the Second Vatican Council.

The Church, therefore, urges her sons *[sic]* to enter with prudence and charity into discussion and collaboration with members of other religions. Let Christians, while witnessing to their own faith and way of life, acknowledge, preserve and encourage the spiritual and moral truths found among non-Christians, also their social life and culture. (Flannery, 1987, 739)

Although some Christians, notably Fundamentalist Evangelicals, do not accept the necessity of interreligious dialogue, the conviction that dialogue between cultures and traditions must be a part of future human understanding is growing. This discussion of Buddhist and Native American religious understandings of the ecological setting of human dignity is intended to be part of such a dialogue.

In the first place, reflection upon the understandings of Buddhists and Native Americans about the interrelatedness of all reality and the dependence of human dignity on this interrelatedness presents both a contrast and enrichment of Christian understandings of the creative act of God as the source for human and natural meaning and dignity. The reflections discussed above raise new perspectives and questions on one's own tradition. To see human dignity from these other perspectives can be an important moment in self-analysis, even though full agreement might not be possible in the last analysis. This interreligious dialogue must be conducted with respect for the integrity and depth of other traditions without compromising one's own.

Christian dialogue with Buddhism is well underway with relation to the important questions of meditation and prayer. On the other hand, dialogue with Buddhists on issues of ecology, human rights, and human dignity have not been pursued with comparable vigor. The discussion above (especially the Strain proposal) are proposed to move this dialogue forward. Dialogue with Native American traditions on ecological issues have garnered more public attention but, unfortunately, often have fallen victim to the stereotyping of Native Americans as "noble savages." There is a need for Christians to delve more deeply into the meaning and variety of Native traditions and their understandings of the role of human beings embedded in the larger order of reality. The elaboration of Native American perspectives above might begin to set this dialogue in the more appropriate context of mutual understanding.

Concretely, how can such a dialogue between Christians, Buddhists, and Native Americans proceed? This is an important challenge presented to Christian communities on the eve of the twenty-first century. Certainly, current dialogues should be continued and expanded to include questions relating not only to spirituality (the present emphasis), but also to the concrete issues that touch the heart of human dignity. Included among these are the issues of ecology and human rights. After such issues are identified and moved more to the center of current religious attention, settings for such dialogue have to be developed if they are not already in place. One possibility is presented by the involvement of diverse religious groups (including Buddhists and Native Americans) in Catholic educational institutions. The experience of educating people from various religious traditions might be a possible foundation for a wider and more respectful dialogue concerning the issues raised in this chapter. More broadly, the American experience of ethnic and cultural diversity might be explored as a foundation for dialogue rather than one of mutual mistrust. Focusing on human dignity (from various cultural and religious perspectives) through discussions of ecology, the environment, and human rights could be a concrete way of bringing religious traditions such as Christianity, Buddhism, and Native traditions into focused and fruitful dialogue. This process can begin in churches, temples, and on reservations without undue delay. The crisis of the environment and threats to human dignity concern all of these traditions and could provide for them an impetus to gather and dialogue. Theological and religious questions will inevitably arise from such conversations. Differing perspectives, even disagreements, will certainly appear. But, most importantly, a kind of mutual religious enrichment will develop in the midst of focusing on some of the most fundamental questions facing the human family at the end of the twentieth century.

NOTE

1. Biblical citations are from NRSV.

REFERENCES

Abe, Masao. "Religious Tolerance and Human Rights: A Buddhist Perspective." *Religious Liberty and Human Rights in Nations and in Religions.* New York: Hippocrene Books, 1986.

Abele, Frances. "Canadian Natives and the Environment." *The Native North American Almanac.* Ed. Duane Champagne. Detroit: Gale Research, Inc., 1994.

Bergant, Dianne, and Carroll Stuhlmueller. "Creation According to the Old Testament." *Evolution and Creation.* Ed. Ernan McMullin. Notre Dame, Ind.: University of Notre Dame Press, 1985, pp. 153–75.

_____. "Is the Biblical World View Anthropocentric?" *New Theology Review* 4 (May 1991): 5–14.

Crowe, Margaret. "U.S. Indians and the Environment." *The Native North American Almanac.* Ed. Duane Champagne. Detroit: Gale Research, Inc., 1994, pp. 593–98.

Dalai Lama. "Human Rights and Universal Responsibility." Talk given at "The United Nations World Conference on Human Rights," Vienna, Austria; June 15, 1993 (http://www.psu.edu/jbe/dalail.html).

Deloria, Vine, Jr. *God Is Red. A Native View of Religion.* Golden, Colo.: Fulcrum Publishing, 1994.

Evans, Santipala Stephen. "Buddhist Resignation and Human Rights." *Journal of Buddhist Ethics.* (Online Conference on Buddhism and Human Rights, 1–14, 1995 (http://www.psu.edu/jbe/evans.txt).

Flannery, O.P., Austin, general ed. *Vatican Council II: The Conciliar and Post-Conciliar Documents.* New Revised Edition. Collegeville, Minn.: The Liturgical Press, 1987.

Gill, Sam D. *Native American Religions. An Introduction.* Belmont, Cal.: Wadsworth Publishing Company, 1982.

_____. *Native American Traditions: Sources and Interpretations.*The Religious Life of Man Series. Belmont, Cal.: Wadsworth Publishing Company, 1983.

Harvey, Peter. *An Introduction to Buddhism: Teachings, History and Practices.* New York: Cambridge University Press, 1990.

Hultkrantz, Ake. *Belief and Worship in Native North America.* Syracuse: Syracuse University Press, 1981.

Inada, Kenneth K. "A Buddhist Response to the Nature of Human Rights." *Asian Perspectives on Human Rights.* Eds. Claude E. Welch, Jr. and Virginia A. Leary. Boulder, Colo.: Westview Press, 1990.

_____. "The Buddhist Perspective on Human Rights." *Human Rights in Religious Traditions.* Ed. Arlene Swidler. New York: Pilgrims Press, 1982, pp. 66–76.

Lal, P. *The Dhammapada.* Noonday. New York: Farrar, Straus & Giroux, 1967.

Mahoney, William K. "Soul: Indian Concept." *The Encyclopedia of Religion,* Volume 13. Ed. Mircea Eliade. New York: Macmillan Publishing Company, 1988.

Malalasekera, G.P. "The Status of the Individual in Theravada Buddhism." *Philosophy East and West* 14 (1964): 145–56.

Mayer, Ann Elizabeth. *Islam and Human Rights: Tradition and Politics.* 2nd Edition. San Francisco: Westview Press, 1995.

Morrison, Kenneth M. "Native American Religions: Creating Through Cosmic Give-and-Take." *The Native North American Almanac.* Detroit: Gale Research, Inc., 1994, pp. 633–48.

Pollis, Adamantia, and Peter Schwab, eds. *Human Rights: Cultural and Ideological Perspectives.* New York: Praeger Publishers, 1979.

Powers, John. "Human Rights and Cultural Values: The Political Philosophies of the Dalai Lama and the People's Republic of China." *Journal of Buddhist Ethics* (Online Conference on Buddhism and Human Rights; October 1–14, 1995 (http://www.psu.edu/jbe/powers.txt).

Sogyal Rinpoche. *The Tibetan Book of Living and Dying.* San Francisco: HarperCollins, 1994.

Strain, Charles R. "Socially Engaged: Buddhism's Contribution to the Transformation of Catholic Social Teachings on Human Rights." *Journal of Buddhist Ethics* (Online Conference on Buddhism and Human Rights, October 1–14, 1995 (http://www.psu.edu/jbe/strain.txt).

Sullivan, Lawrence E. *Icanchu's Drum: An Orientation to Meaning in South American Religions*. New York: Macmillan Publishing Company, 1988.

United Nations. *The Universal Declaration of Human Rights* (Online Conference on Buddhism and Human Rights; October 1–14, 1995 (http://www.psu.edu/jbe/declarn.html).

Vecsey, Christopher. "American Indian Environmental Religions." *American Indian Environments: Ecological Issues in Native American History*. Eds. Christopher and Robert W. Vanables. Syracuse: Syracuse University Press, 1980, pp, 1–37.

The Threat of Commodity-Consciousness to Human Dignity

Ron DiSanto

> *The world is too much with us; late and soon,*
> *Getting and spending, we lay waste our powers;*
> *Little we see in Nature that is ours;*
> *We have given our hearts away, a sordid boon!*
> *— "The World Is Too Much with Us"*
> William Wordsworth

If there was some truth to these words at the time of Wordsworth, that truth is especially worth noting and repeating today. Since then, commercial activity ("getting" and "spending") has increased dramatically. For too many of us, buying and selling has become a way of life. In our current environment, then, perhaps the case must be made that a focus on such activity involves a waste—a waste of human powers and a despoilment and divestiture of the human heart.

Such a focus on commercialist values is a threat to human dignity, a threat that is dangerous insofar as it is not perceived as a threat. Let it be clear that the following argument concerns a *mentality* pervading our culture, and not commercial activity as such. Clearly, we need material goods, the money that buys them, and the activity by which goods and money are procured. We are not spirits; we cannot do without things. Taoists and others advocating the value of simplicity remind us that we do not need as many things as we think we do. And yet need is part of our material condition. What we do *not* need is a mentality that cajoles us into degrading ourselves and others. In this chapter *commodity-consciousness* will be contrasted with *love-consciousness*.

In the first section commodity-consciousness will be defined as an improper focus on commercial activity. In the second, the nature of human dignity will be discussed in terms of the proper actuation of higher human powers. It will be within this context that the mentality of love-consciousness is contrasted with commodity-consciousness. The third section of the chapter will show how commodity-consciousness (born of the marriage between capitalism and technology) constitutes a threat to human dignity. Finally, there will be some proposals for how we might begin to address the threat that commodity-consciousness poses.

I. THE MEANING OF COMMODITY-CONSCIOUSNESS

Basically, to describe commodity-consciousness as a mentality is to see it as a complex of beliefs and attitudes that center on *the pursuit of useful, buyable things and of the purchasing power that gets them.*

Being "centered" implies that not just any degree of concern will do since, obviously, most of us living in society must show some degree of concern for things and for money. But this is not the same as making these things central, or being gripped by commodity-consciousness.

The phrase "useful, buyable things" is more or less synonymous with *commodity*, as that word is used in this chapter. Sometimes the word *commodity* is used in a broad sense to denote anything that is useful or convenient in any way, since the Latin root of the word is *commodus,* which means "convenient" or "useful." But the term also has associations with economic activity. (The *American Heritage Desk Dictionary* points out that one usage connects a "commodity" with a "commercial advantage"; *Websters New Collegiate Dictionary* offers "economic good" as one meaning of "commodity.") Then, by definition for the purposes here, something like "sunshine," however useful and convenient it may be, is not a commodity in the designated sense, in economic parlance, "nonrivalrous" and "nonexcludable"—it cannot be bottled and sold.

The phrase "purchasing power" obviously refers to both money and credit. But money is also a commodity, since it also has value, or is buyable. Indeed, it might be thought of as the ultimate commodity, since its range of usefulness is as vast as the range of what can be bought.

Who will be the example of someone "consumed" by this kind of consciousness? How will he or she think or act? Will he or she quest only for the perfect mall? Perhaps this kind of person is like someone we all know. If, for instance, a man takes three jobs to support himself far beyond basic needs, and takes up all his time doing so, or if a woman plays the stock market and her cellular phone is worn like some earring, then these people may be consumed by the process. Whatever form it may take, a salient characteristic of this mentality, for present purposes, is *insatiability:* wanting more and more.

And the needy consumer can rest assured that the well of commodities, of new and better things to be bought, will not dry up. By the marriage of capitalism to technology—given the inner élan of each— there is a guarantee that an ever-increasing number and variety of goods will flow from the well. As long as individuals maintains a focus on commodity fulfillment, they will never be satisfied and will never reach a point where they cease to go after more and more of the same.

So to the extent that this desire for more and more commodity fulfillment takes hold, one's whole world will be colored by this desire. As a result, a person is increasingly likely to think of fellow human beings as parts of the "commoditized" world or as means to an end. Other people will become "contacts" and "connections" that will assure full entry into the garden of commodity-fulfillment, even if the consumer has to purchase them with some sort of more or less beguiling interaction. (This mentality of commodity-consciousness once adopted bids us to believe everything has its price.)

By so doing, commodity-consciousness will have thus taken a new turn. To the first dimension of commodity-consciousness, the tendency to think of fulfillment in terms of the acquisition of commodities, will have been added a second dimension: the tendency to regard human beings themselves as commodities to be bought and used. The inner dynamic of commodity-consciousness can be seen as a cycle revolving around these two dimensions or poles. The more one is fascinated with money and commodities, the more one is led to instrumentalize and commoditize human beings (oneself as well as others). The more we commoditize and thereby degrade human beings, the easier it becomes for us to overvalue commodities. And so on.

The behavior of particular persons will fit this description only to the extent that the inner dynamic is given full release. If this is the case, then a viewpoint emerges in the form of a person who will be referred to in the present context as "Comcon."

Comcon looks at the world of buyable things as a garden of inexhaustible delights. Comcon enters this garden and seeks to taste everything it offers. Since the garden is huge and nothing in it is free, in order to continue the universal tasting tour, Comcon has to earn a lot of money. Comcon comes to see that other people in the garden can be used to Comcon's advantage. They can be hired to pick the fruit. They can also be cajoled into taking Comcon to parts of the garden that Comcon otherwise would not reach. They may be companions in the tasting of the garden's fruits, provided they do not stand in the way of Comcon's project. But when people, as they sometimes do, get in the way, then they must be dealt with cleverly. People can come and go; it's the garden that matters.

After a period of time, Comcon has tasted quite a bit and even come to own much of the garden. But there is still much, much more to taste and to produce and to own. But time is running out. Efforts will have to be doubled and redoubled. People will have to be dealt with and used even more cleverly.

Comcon's mentality, I will argue, poses a threat to human dignity, to Comcon's own dignity as well as to the dignity of other fruit-tasters and fruit-pickers and fruit-producers. It poses a threat to those who, like Comcon, think the garden is the only place to be and thus are consumed by it. It certainly poses a threat to those who would attempt to make their way out of the garden, seeking only to visit as need arises. But before discussing this further, it is necessary to describe the human nature that is threatened.

II. THE NATURE OF HUMAN DIGNITY

The word *dignity* is rooted in the Latin word *dignus,* which means "worthy." So to ask about human dignity is to ask about human "worthiness" or "worth" and to invoke a certain relativity. Worthy of whom? Of What? And in whose eyes? Worth in relation to what standard? Worth for whom?

Let us assume that human beings have a certain worth, at least for themselves, simply by being the *kind* of being they are. Let us also assume that this kind of basic dignity or worth that comes with being a member of the species is compounded when humans actuate themselves in appropriate ways. Given these assumptions, the question about where my dignity lies becomes two questions: What kind of beings are we? How do we appropriately express the kind of beings we are?

Different answers are, of course, possible, and in the history of thought, different answers have been given. At least one thing is clear: Anyone who has bothered to attempt an answer has made use of higher conscious powers. Without the use of such powers, the question itself could not be grasped or cared about, much less answered. Minimally speaking, then, a human being is an emotional, intellectual being with volitional powers. As humans we care about things, come to understand them, think things through, and make decisions.

Although there is no need to take a Cartesian stand, what is proposed has that kind of ring to it, for it was the seventeenth-century thinker, René Descartes (1596–1650), who noted that his certainty about his own existence was connected with his certainty that he was a "a thing that thinks." He included in this activity the whole gamut of human consciousness—perception and imagination as well as thinking and feeling and willing.

Consider Aristotle (384–322 B.C.) whose response to the question, "What kind of being is a human being?" was that a human being is a "rational animal." In this view, rationality, more than anything else, is what makes the specifically human and gives human dignity.

Consider also the view of Immanuel Kant (1724-1804) who held that the only thing of unconditional worth is a "good will," thus associating this quality with human dignity or worth. He meant by this not blind assertive power, but rather the capacity to make decisions and direct one's living on the basis of reason. For him this capacity was located in our intellectual and volitional consciousness, but in *Critique of Judgment* he discusses the importance of human imagination and feeling. Thus, for Kant, too, being human means being conscious imaginally, emotionally, intellectually, and volitionally.

Finally, consider the biblical view that a human being is a child of God, made in the image and likeness of God (see the chapter by James Scullion). Is a human being a child of God in a way that a butterfly or a stone is not? If so, then what is special about a human being? Is it our capacity to love? Even though there may be a kind of love we share with the rest of the animal kingdom, it would seem there is a specifically human form of love that involves our imagination, our emotions, our intellect, and our volitional consciousness.

So, if we suppose these things, one might conclude that any threat to a person's capacity to imagine or feel or think or will is a threat to his or her dignity. If anything diminishes one or more of these capacities, it diminishes human dignity. If anything eradicates one or more of them, it eradicates human dignity. And if anything tempts us to ignore the development and fulfillment of the capacities to imagine, feel, think, and will, it is a temptation to violate our human dignity.

Before beginning a full-scale discussion of how commodity-consciousness threatens us in this way, a second question must be addressed: How do people appropriately express what they are? What happens if people think or feel, for instance, in wrong ways or to wrong ends? Is there a right way to actuate our higher powers? And is there some given end or set of ends, built into my human condition, that provides a standard for determining whether or not we actuate our powers in the right ways?

These are big questions that many say are beyond the capacity of reason to answer. Liberal individualists, for example, say that we should be individually free to determine our ends since these questions are impervious to reason. Fideists say that we can answer them only on the basis of faith. They are certainly right if the work of reason is understood, in the manner of Cartesian rationalism, as the attainment of an absolute, geometric-like certainty. But as Aristotle noted (in Book One of the *Nichomachean Ethics*), we should not expect more certainty in an inquiry than a given area of investigation allows.

So, then, discussion about ends or, more generally, value-talk requires being rational without being geometric and must involve some kind of fusion between subjectivity and objectivity. For, clearly, the context of practical living calls for engagement as well as reasonableness. In practical living, we are called to be neither unthinking emotive reactors nor detached thinking machines.

To live at the fusion point of subjectivity and objectivity is to open oneself up, without taking leave of thought, to the gamut of human experience and to the feelings evoked therein. From this thoughtful and feeling-filled self-opening there can emerge insights about human ends that are *practically* verifiable, that is, insights that are validated in practice through the peace and joy that they bring. One such insight is that we are here to learn how to love, that love is central to human living, that in widening and deepening and actuating our capacity to love we move more and more toward fulfillment.

Christians will find this insight to be in accord with the central teaching of Christianity. To follow Jesus is to live a life of love, thereby becoming ever more a child of God. The call expressed in the Great

Commandment is to love God with one's whole heart and soul and mind and to love one's neighbor as oneself. God, neighbor, and self are thus seen as proper objects of love. To this list, we might add the earth's non-human inhabitants, for, as those who attend animals or plants know, there is a certain peace and joy found in this expression of love as well.

A. Love-Consciousness

But what is love? Plato (427-347 B.C.) provides a good starting point for addressing this question. In his *Symposium,* Plato has Socrates speak of eros, or love, as an orientation of our being toward ever higher forms of the good and the beautiful. Human beings are drawn to these qualities insofar as we ourselves have a certain lack in regard to them; we are neither totally good nor totally beautiful. And in allowing ourselves to be drawn, we seek to unite with the good that is outside ourselves and to fill up what is lacking in ourselves. In Socrates' account of eros, the ascent of love is from physical goodness or beauty to spiritual goodness or beauty, from the love of bodies to the love of minds and social institutions and knowledge, and, at the limit, the Good (which is more or less the Platonic equivalent of the religious notion of God).

A couple of things are worth noting about this. First, love inevitably involves *self-love.* In seeking to possess, become one with, and generate through the varied forms of the good and the beautiful that we find outside ourselves, the dimension of self-love is never entirely lacking. Second, for Plato, this drive toward self-fulfillment requires an upward movement—the eros that is central to our being will be frustrated if it is forced to stay focused on lower levels of the good and the beautiful. So the trick is not to get stuck.

Now it may be noted, by way of contrast, that commodity-consciousness is horizontal rather than vertical. Individuals are deceived into thinking that fulfillment will come by way of their continuing to roam about the garden rather than climbing out of the garden into the foothills and mountains of human aspiration.

So Platonic love is thus a desire-based love that moves people toward fulfillment by ever raising the level of desires. And growing up (if this is to be understood qualitatively and not merely quantitatively) is, after all, largely a matter of educating desire and transforming it to ever higher levels, including that level whereon one finds fulfillment by making a social contribution.

B. Christian Perspectives on Love

However, human experience and Christian belief also point to the insufficiency of this kind of love. If we are supposed to love our neighbor as ourselves, then we ought to seek the good and fulfillment of the neighbor as well as the good and fulfillment of ourselves. Here enters, then, the Christian notion of agape, a kind of love that can be contrasted with Platonic eros. Whereas eros is drawn *upward,* toward a good that will fulfill oneself, agape reaches *outward and downward* toward whatever is lacking in others, responds positively to this lack, and seeks thereby the fulfillment of others. The model for this, in the Christian scheme of things, is God's love for the world, for God's love is not motivated by any lack in God. God does not love the world as a route to self-fulfillment. God loves the world to fulfill the world; and God calls and empowers human beings to love the same way.

1. Eros and Agape

While it is possible to draw a contrast between eros and agape in an extreme way that forces a choice between the two as between two radically different lifestyles, there is really no more contradiction between the two than there is between self-love and other-love. A life centered on self-fulfillment can be contrasted with a life of self-denial and self-sacrifice for the sake of others. An orientation toward association with people who have a lot going for them, whether it be beauty or talent or achievement or some other amiable quality, can be contrasted with an orientation toward association with, for example, the poor, the needy, the physically or mentally impaired, the socially marginalized. And we are sometimes confronted with hard choices between these two poles. But there is nothing self-contradictory in the idea that a loving person can be both erosic and agapic, and there is much to recommend both the view of eros and agape as complementary and the conscious attempt to live this complementarity.

Thus, at one moment humans can allow themselves to be drawn erosically toward what is good and beautiful, thus loving themselves as well as the good toward which they are drawn; at the next moment, they can allow themselves to be stirred by the neighbor's need and to reach out agapically to help, thus loving another. No contradiction. All in a day's life.

Not only is there no contradiction between eros and agape; there is something suspect about the idea that either can stand by itself in the life of a mature human being. Consider, first, eros without agape. Imagine someone totally and exclusively gripped by erosic drive toward self-fulfillment, a "self-actualizer" who, unfortunately, is incapable or unwilling to respond to the pains and needs of others. Just as we might be charmed by a child that needs to grow up, we might also be charmed by this sort of "self-actualizer" but not fooled into thinking such a person an adult.

Consider, next, agape without eros. Imagine a person totally and exclusively gripped by a will to respond to the pains and needs of other human beings, a person who takes no delight in anything good or beautiful, a person without interests or joys. Perhaps some may be tempted to think of such a person not as stunted, like the exclusively erosic person, but as saintly. The temptation should be resisted. A genuine saint, so far from being devoid of eros, is in love with God. Not only does this erosic love motivate the saint to respond to the pains and needs of others (agape); it also colors the saint's perception of the world, allowing the saint to appreciate goodness and beauty (eros) where others would not. So while the agapic love of a saint is erosically charged, the exclusively agapic love of a pseudo-saint is rather a symptom of illness.

If love-consciousness can be divided into eros and agape, the division should be seen as one between complementary dimensions rather than antagonistic types. Eros and agape are more wisely viewed as dancing partners than as boxing opponents.

2. Another Distinction: Appreciation and Concern

Along similar lines, love-consciousness can be split into appreciation and concern. When people love appreciatively, say in the context of a masterful artistic performance, they are taken up with the presence of goodness or beauty. They say yes to that goodness or beauty, and to whatever has it. And when they love concernedly, say in the context of a friend's emotional suffering, they are taken up with the absence of something good or beautiful in that person. They say "no" to that absence. They want to fill it. They may take pains to do so.

Since, in human life, the good is never wholly present or wholly absent, one can count on appreciation-love and concern-love to take turns. However, this rhythm is not the whole story. Like the *yin* and the *yang* of Chinese thought, appreciation and concern call for each other, flow into each other, mutually energize each other. Appreciation-love of the arts may evoke a concern about their lack of support, thus causing a patron to give in that direction. Or appreciation of a particular achievement may evoke a concern about an undernourished part of the self, thus evoking more attention to its lack.

Individuals cannot love erosically (or appreciatively or in a *yin* mode) without opening up the self and apprehending the goodness and beauty of someone or something. Such apprehension may occur on the level of the senses, but, at least on the higher levels of erosic receptivity, it will also involve opening up the channels of feeling and thinking. The will also will be involved, for when an individual is erosically engaged, he or she definitely wants something: minimally, the person wants to continue to enjoy the presence of whatever has stimulated the eros (for example, a beautiful piece of music one does not want to end). If it is possible to be united further with what is loved, the individual will want that as well, and this may be a springboard to resolute action. For example, Herculean efforts toward winning another's heart can follow the experience of falling in love.

People cannot engage agapically (or concernedly or in a *yang* mode) without engaging their cognitive powers. An active effort to relieve the pain, heal a wound, remedy a defect, or, in general, make things better involves an attempt to understand both the problem and its solution. This attempt may well call for the actuation of powers of feeling and imagining as well as thinking power. And of course, by definition, agapic loving will involve the summoning of will power to make the absent good present.

Thus, when love-consciousness is operating, the higher human powers are operating, and they are operating each in its own way toward the *good*. What is "good"? Abstract formulaic answers have been offered, but none will be offered here. The point is rather that love-consciousness moves us in that direction by summoning and actuating our powers both to *understand*, more clearly and thoroughly and more deeply, and to *will*, more resolutely and more efficaciously, what is good. There is a process here. It's like being on a train. As long as people do not get stopped or derailed, they will get where they need to be. Love-consciousness fuels the train.

III. The Threat of Commodity-Consciousness

It is necessary to examine more explicitly how commodity-consciousness constitutes a threat to human dignity, a force that can stop or derail the train of human development as it is fueled by love-consciousness, by eros and agape. To the extent that human beings are gripped by commodity-consciousness, their focus is not on the development of their higher powers but on the accumulation of things. And it follows that they seek fulfillment not by learning to love in progressively deeper and broader ways but by becoming thing-acquirers, toy-gatherers, fruit-tasters. This focus is an affront to human dignity, a sort of saying no to what the humans are (high-powered lovers) and a settling for being less than what humans are (pleasure-driven tasters or convenience-and-comfort addicts).

But the affront to human dignity does not stop here. This focus can easily pull people into practices and lifestyles that involve the tendency to think of other human beings not as centers of agapic concern but as obstacles (competing fruit-tasters) to the self's pursuits, or as resources (buyable fruit-pickers) to be used in such pursuits, or as annoying detractors possessing voices that must be silenced less they be heard.

The task is to refuel the love-train, but this can not be done until the person dispels the mesmerizing effects of commodity-consciousness. And this requires breaking the spell, and becoming fully aware of all of its guises and its contemporary manifestations in our capitalist, technological society. For this is where its presence and its threat are especially pervasive and insidious. First, however, a look at the perennial aspect of the threat is in order.

A. Perennial Aspect

It is safe to say that greed is a perennial temptation and a perennial problem for the human condition. It is not just the poor whom we have always with us; not so coincidentally the greedy have always been there, too. Since Genesis there have always been human beings who wanted much more than they needed, who strove to accumulate much more than they needed, and who treated other human beings either as obstacles to their pursuits or as potential instruments in their attainment.

Where others are regarded as obstacles, the task is to get them out of the way. This can be accomplished through a variety of ways, such as deceit, bribery, blackmail, and murder. When people are considered instruments, the task is to make full and profitable use of them, which again can be, and has been, accomplished in a variety of ways, including deceit, bribery, blackmail, and slavery. In either case, it is not hard to see that a form of commodity-consciousness has taken hold: Things have become focal and people have become things. A distorted view of human fulfillment has taken over, one that threatens the human dignity both of the truncated person who looks through such a lens and of the objectified persons who are seen through this lens.

Slavery is one of the most dramatic forms in which another human is viewed as "property" and turned into a commodity to be used or exchanged. It is also a clear example of the two dimensions of commodity-consciousness merging. For the tendency to think of one's own fulfillment in terms of amassing commodities becomes, *directly,* the tendency to commoditize other human beings.

B. Contemporary Aspect

Greed and enslavement are thus perennial forms of commodity-consciousness, and, in the contemporary situation, the social complex created by the union of capitalism and technology enlarges both their scope and their intensity. The capitalist greed for money must be matched by a consumer greed for commodable things. The tendency to enslave and use other human beings takes on subtler forms and becomes more prevalent as technology opens up newer possibilities for use and abuse.

There is, however, a counter-claim to the argument that commodity-consciousness deadens or misuses the higher human powers, especially with regard to technological advancement. Celebrators of capitalism as well of technology may say that the world of commodity-consciousness is populated by some very intelligent high achievers, people who are well developed and self-actuated, and who, because they are strong-willed and intelligent, go on to develop themselves further because they are driven by commodity-consciousness. In fact, there might be a nice cycle here, with human development and commodity-consciousness reinforcing each other.

Not untypically, when a capitalist is confronted with the idea that capitalism puts profits above people and, thereby, creates or contributes to unconscionable gaps between rich and poor, haves and have-nots, the capitalist responds that capitalism, along with technology, has created a world of undreamed-of comforts and conveniences, of ingenious labor-saving and life-extending devices, of mind-boggling extensions of the human capacities of movement and communication. And this has been achieved through the profit motive, for it is the profit motive that has inspired and stimulated human ingenuity and inventiveness. It is the profit motive that has created the garden of delights in which we now live. Does anyone seriously want to leave this garden and return to the precapitalist desert, with all of its drudgery and misery and monotony and premature death?

Thus, in this view, the profit motive is not a form of greed, or if it is, then greed can be a good thing. The defender of commodity-consciousness would likely take issue with the idea that the garden may be inimical to human development and the actuation of higher human powers.

Moreover, there is a happy marriage between the capitalist defender of the profit motive and the defender of commodity-consciousness. The defender of the profit motive wants to maintain the stream of new goods, and the defender of commodity-consciousness wants the commodities to keep coming. Both thrive on the sharpening of human ingenuity; both are glad about the garden of delights that results therefrom.

By way of response it is useful to raise two questions. Is it possible to criticize capitalism and, at the same time and without self-contradiction, acknowledge the many benefits that a capitalist economy (or, more accurately, a mixed economy) has produced? And is it possible to decry commodity-consciousness and, at the same time and without self-contradiction, acknowledge that there are many commodities worth pursuing?

The answer to both questions is affirmative. There is no contradiction between acknowledging capitalism's benefits and also noting its shortcomings.

To say that one must embrace capitalism totally or not at all is to commit the black-or-white fallacy and invite a form of idolatry. A person can be grateful for the benefits that a capitalist system has made available and at the same time reject its theoretical underpinnings (e.g., the view of neoclassical economists who viewed human beings as irreformably selfish and given to insatiable wants). Without removing all support for capitalism the critic can call for structural remedies for its shortcomings and call attention to the threat to human dignity that occurs when the profit motive is made central to human life and promoted as in the myth of "The American Dream."

Similarly, an individual can welcome a variety of useful commodities and choose to use them with *discernment*. More importantly, the critic can reject the idea that such a flow of goods represents the totality of "the good life." One should neither totally embrace not totally discard all commodities and all claims for the capitalist system in which we live. Instead, one can be wary of a kind of consciousness that involves a false, and ultimately an empty, vision of human happiness and thereby short-circuits our movement toward full humanness and human fulfillment.

1. Commodity-Consciousness and Human Fulfillment

Let it be granted that because of commodity-consciousness (and the profit motive) human beings have exerted and extended themselves, unleashed their imaginations, had creative insights, made full use of their deliberative powers, planned carefully, and carried out projects with determination and self-discipline. And let it be granted, that in so doing, they have actuated higher human powers. And that, as such, is a good thing. Does it follow from this that the people who are thus engaged are, by that very fact, bringing about the human fulfillment of *others* who will taste the fruits of their efforts? Does it follow that they are fulfilling *themselves* as human beings? The answer to both questions is negative. Neither the fruit-producer nor the fruit-taster, in this context, if you assume they are gripped by commodity-consciousness, can attain human fulfillment.

The first problem is that commodities that require a good deal of imagination, creativity, and planning for their successful production do not necessarily require a high level of actuation of human powers on the receiving end by those who procure and use them.

There is usually an asymmetry between commodity-production and commodity-reception that is part of the lure of the commodity. The sweat and thought that go into the commodity's production relieve the user of sweat and thought on the other end. For instance, people use lawn mowers and automatic dishwashers to *decrease* the work required in the performance of the tasks involved. An awesome mental accomplishment might lie behind the production of a simple electronic calculator, but it does not take awesome mental powers to use one. In fact (and here the worm in the apple begins to show itself), one who relies upon such a commodity may lose or may never acquire certain arithmetical capabilities. Something may have been gained, but something is lost as well. Even though someone may not need the lost capabilities, he or she should not be deceived into thinking that by making the self thus dependent one is functioning at a higher level.

It is important to understand the trade-offs that are made. These may take the form of a lessening of personal functioning, and, of course, this is not a new insight. Over two millennia ago Plato noted in the *Phaedrus* that writing will bring forgetfulness to human souls. Fortunately Plato did not, because of this, refrain from writing. But the truth of what he says stands, for it is true that human memory is stronger in an oral culture than in a scriptoral culture. So while the possibilities opened up by a new technology may be awesome, the potential losses in human functioning should not be ignored because of some utopian faith in technological advancement.

Consider also the gains that have been made in the technology of travel. Are they pure, unadulterated gains with no losses attached? Do the later and better forms of travel ensure the full actuation of human powers? A man can go farther and faster by automobile than he can go by bicycle, but if he wants to keep his legs from turning into jelly, sooner or later he will have to get out of the car to use them. Once again, gains *and* losses. Ivan Illich has said that even the claim that the man goes faster by automobile is questionable, once we factor in the hours he needs to put into money-earning activity in order to attain and maintain the automobile. People must be on guard against thinking that new and better commodities will make life better in all respects. (As the old General Electric slogan put it, "Better products for better living.") Such thinking is part of the mythic delusion of commodity-consciousness.

2. Television and Commodity-Consciousness

Now consider the example of television. While it is possible to *use* television as a stimulus for the actuation of one's higher powers, it is hardly the case that this sort of use is required, expected, or even commonplace. The expression "couch potato," although it may be used humorously, betrays the reality that spending a lot of time in front of the television involves the diminution of human powers. It might not be the case that one is a total vegetable; a variety of images and thoughts may move across one's mental screen. But what is lost is not just opportunity costs. The images and thoughts have been produced by *another.* The "couch potato" who has made television viewing a way of life is more likely to have developed her capacity to be mesmerized than to have developed her capacity to use her higher human powers in an active manner. Passivity tends to go with the territory.

In a situation of passivity, the threat to human dignity is compounded, for the viewer not only is cajoled into accepting a lower level of functioning but also is put in a highly programmable state. In fact, as a viewer, she may end up with an internal program of which she is not even aware. One such program is certainly the very complex of beliefs and attitudes that constitutes commodity-consciousness.

If one doubts that television does a good job of programming people in this direction, one need only pay attention to the high cost of television advertising: in 1997, a second of television time during the Superbowl cost $40,000. This amount of money is not paid because advertising does not work.

But what does it mean to say that advertising is effective? It means that when an individual has "bought into" a vision of human fulfillment that centers on the accumulation of commodities (the first level of commodity-consciousness) she is reduced by this particular commodity (i.e., television) to a quasi-commoditized state (the second level of commodity-consciousness) and, while in this state, she is manipulated into buying something she does not need with money she may not have.

3. The Computer as an Exception?

Now a potential counter-example: The computer seems to represent so much of what is right about contemporary technology. For instance, it has opened up the possibility of a worldwide web of users and thus contributed to the ideal of a global village in which people of different cultures come to know and to access one another ever more quickly and effectively.

Unlike the way television is used, the computer is an interactive device. Use of a computer requires more than merely turning it on or flicking channels. Interaction with a computer requires at least minimal use of higher human powers. And, depending on what program is used, the level of interaction may, in fact, be quite high. For instance, meeting the challenge of a computer game may require high use of the imagination as well as logical powers. (The computer games *Civilization* and *Simm City* come to mind here since their object is to build, from scratch, a civilization or a city, respectively.) Also, by using a computer to construct a graph or a spreadsheet, someone can assess needs and resources and, even, potential solutions to problems. In such a use one may stretch the imagination, have an implosion of insight, or even increase logical skills.

The computer as a word processing tool affords an author conveniences and possibilities far beyond those of the typewriter. The writer can play with the computer in a way one could never play with the typewriter, and such play is the parent of insight. This is indeed a tool that can be used to actuate higher human powers.

However, the pertinent word is *can*. While the computer can be used in ways that heighten one's powers, there is no necessity that it be used in such a way. It can also be used in a way that invites people to waste their powers. For there is also the kind of game available on computer that provides no more than a minimal challenge to eye-hand coordination and a maximal invitation to spend endless hours in mindless "fun."

Aside from games, if an individual plugs into the Internet, he or she can access a great deal of information, but also a great number of buying and selling opportunities. The "information highway" may provide people with opportunities for learning, but one can also expect to find on this highway innumerable opportunities for developing or reinforcing commodity-consciousness. And, given that this highway and the computers that have been designed to access it have been created in a capitalist context, this comes as no surprise.

While computers and computer packages may offer opportunities for the development of the higher human powers, they do so in the context of commodity-consciousness, and they are designed not to do away with this context but to reinforce it, and even to expand it. So, just as the highways along which people travel in their automobiles are dotted with exits to "outlet centers" where they can exercise the desire to shop, the information highway can be expected to be dotted with exits to a wide variety of markets. And just as the outlet centers both result from and contribute to the density of travel along the auto highways, so too the markets accessed by the information highway will increase as travel along this highway increases, and, concomitantly, travel will increase along this highway as the accessible markets increase. The market mentality is alive and well. The profit motive thrives.

Does this mean the computer is a bad thing? No. It simply means that the computer, despite its promise, is not a tool that will, of itself, take us beyond the confines of commodity-consciousness and cause us to actuate fully our higher human powers, transporting us to the peaks of human fulfillment. The computer can be a tool to actuate the functioning of our higher powers, but the mere functioning of these powers is not enough. For, if we are to reach the mountaintops, it is not enough that our higher powers are engaged—they need to be engaged unto the right things.

If the computer engages humankind's higher powers toward the pursuit of the commodity-vision of human fulfillment, it will have contributed not to human liberation but to enslavement. And as willing captives, people will continue to degrade themselves by centering on toy gathering and by thinking of human fulfillment in those terms. Individuals will also be tempted to degrade others by regarding them either as competitors to be defeated or as toys themselves. *And enslavement will be all the stronger insofar as a person is deluded into thinking that he or she is functioning at a higher level.*

But just as an intelligent, creative, and self-disciplined burglar who works the homes of the wealthy is still a burglar, so a highly functioning slave of commodity-consciousness is still a slave. With high levels of technology used unconsciously with no attention to their costs, including the opportunity costs involved in their use, the threat to human dignity has not been abated but compounded. For to the illusion of commodity-fulfillment has been added the illusion of high-level functioning.

4. To What End?

Now to return, once again, to the case of the "fruit-producer" who may be creative, insightful, reflective, and determined. Perhaps this person is wealthy and respected because of contributions made to the world of commodities. Because this person has developed strong habits of mental functioning, the "fruit-producer" may not dwell indolently in the garden of delights, but, instead, continue to stretch the higher human powers. Does not such a dynamic and successful person illustrate the fact that commodity-consciousness and genuinely high-level functioning go hand in hand?

If there is a simple equation of high-level functioning with the talented use of higher powers, whatever the ends involved, the answer is yes. But what if one attends to ends? As Kant pointed out, "talents of mind" and "qualities of temperament" that are good in many respects may still be used in bad and harmful ways if "good will" is lacking (*Groundwork,* 1964, 393). To use a non-Kantian example, suppose a hired killer makes effective use of the "talents of mind" and "qualities of temperament" to which Kant refers, and becomes a "good" hired killer. In the process, he will actuate and perhaps develop these powers and qualities. But such a person will not be a *good person* nor will the powers and capabilities he uses be unqualifiedly good. Speaking abstractly, if we forget what the "hit man" is doing and focus only upon the level of mental intensity involved, we might be tempted to say that the skilled hit man is functioning at a "high level"; but if we look at the situation concretely and consider what the hit man is about, the temptation vanishes.

In the present context, then, it is important to attend more carefully to what the highly functioning and effective fruit-producer is doing. If such a person is centrally focused on making money, and if such a focus is not appropriately central to human life (because what *is* central is the development of love), it can be said that such a person lacks "good will" and is inappropriately oriented and, therefore, despite appearances, is not fully functioning as a human being.

To live such a life is to threaten one's own dignity, and if one's way of life is both contributing to the commodity-consciousness of other people and, worse, treating other people as themselves commodities to be used or exchanged, then one poses a threat to the human dignity of others as well.

At this point in the argument it is necessary to focus a bit more closely on the specific contributions of capitalism and technology to the malaise of commodity-consciousness. Although each will be looked at in turn, it is impossible to focus on either one without bringing in the other; and from this it should become clear that the two together, acting as a united force, have a power that goes beyond the simple addition of isolated factors.

IV. MAKING THE CONNECTIONS

A. The Link with Capitalism

With regard to capitalism, three things will be examined: the profit motive, competition, and employment practices. First, consider what has already been said about something that lies at the heart of capitalism, the profit motive. If profits are to continue and increase, markets must not only be maintained, but also expanded. In a competitive context, the maintenance of markets requires either the continual "improvement" of offered products or shifts to brand new products or lines of products. As to the expansion of markets, barring the colonization of other planets, this cannot go on indefinitely in a geographic sense, so, sooner or later, it will have to go on in an intensive sense, by the introduction of brand new commodities in preexisting markets. Thus, marketing creates demand. But the most important thing that advertising must condition people to want, if the indefinite, intensive expansion of markets is to be effective, is commodity-fulfillment itself.

People must be hooked on the belief that they can purchase happiness. Once people are hooked on this belief, the rest is easy. Commodity-consciousness will have made them eager to be swayed by the charms of advertising technology. Advertisement will have itself become a drug whose daily dose is craved and demanded. ("Give us this day our daily advertisement!")

Consider next the contribution to commodity-consciousness that comes from another facet of capitalism, the emphasis placed on competition. In addition to the competition among producers for consumers, there is a competition among potential employees for jobs and positions that pay well or have other desirable benefits attached to them. And to attain such jobs and positions, potential employees have to "package" themselves and present themselves as superior to other candidates. This self-packaging is a form of self-commoditization. To carry out the self-sale effectively, the would-be employee may want to purchase commodities designed to aid in this process, such as books and tapes or the resources of a career counselor. For there are commodities for everything, including the process of self-commoditization.

There is a danger that this self-commoditization in the context of seeking employment will turn into something more pervasive: *the general belief that who one is, after all, is the package that one is taught to pre-sent—the objectified, commoditized version of oneself.* So, instead of viewing the self as a person who is on a journey, a person who has experienced much and has much more to experience, a person who has come to understand some things and has much more to understand, a person who has loved and has much more loving to do, we will think of ourselves as the abstract, frozen version, the persona of our achievements, as something that can be reduced to a resume or advertisement.

In this scenario the individual now is dependent on the marketplace for any sense of self-worth. If the individual happens to be one of the "winners" in this context, things may seem to work out well, and the person will have a strong sense of self-worth. However, this sense of self-worth may become too strong and turn into arrogance; and, since the seeds of self-worth have been planted in the shallow soil of commodity-consciousness, the roots will be weak and the flowers not long-lasting. In the end, one is found to be in a state of self-loathing.

On the other hand, if the individual happens to be one of the "losers" in the self-commodity sale, the person may already be in such a state. It is no wonder that, in a context thus permeated by commodity-consciousness, there is so much talk about "self-esteem" needs and "self-esteem" problems.

Finally, it is instructive to look at employment practices in a capitalist context. Obviously, job performance is a factor in determining whether a person will keep a job or lose it. Clearly, the competent performance of employees can contribute to money-making, and for that reason competent people should be hired and paid at a level that keeps them willing and happy to work. But what if staying in the money-making business and keeping up with (or ahead of) the competition requires "restructuring" or "downsizing" or replacing people with computers? At that point, competence and performance often become irrelevant and highly competent people can lose their jobs. Although those people doing the dismissing may not be uncaring, the bottom line must be considered in such a system, and the bottom line is that employees are regarded as commodities to begin with—as commodity-producing commodities—and, like all commodities, are discardable. To the extent that the dismissed employees have themselves "bought into" this commodity-consciousness, they will, again, equate their self-worth with their commodity-value and they will suffer not only economically, but psychologically.

But it is not only those who lose their jobs who suffer from this dehumanizing tendency of capitalism; it is also those who keep their jobs but are forced to work, for lack of better available alternatives, at extremely low wages or under highly stressful or even deplorable conditions. For instance, how many people can live decently on a minimum wage? Not only is this still a contemporary problem in spite of improvements, it is a phenomenon that is especially prevalent in the Third World where multinational corporations exploit "cheap" labor and lax regulatory environments. There it is easy to find sweatshops and child-labor and other forms of indignity that we might associate with a Dickens novel. In the mid-1990s, the Nike Corporation offered an example of this that caught the media's eyes. For a short period of time, Nike came under the shadow of moral judgment, but within a year it was back to business as usual, and Nike's star shown as brightly as ever, with the endorsements of such athletic superstars as Michael Jordan.

It is painful to be attentive to this sort of thing. People may prefer to think that all the commodities that lie within their price range have stayed there because of the magic of technology. Certainly technology has played its part, but so has the lack of a world-wide union movement and the concomitant treatment of human beings as commodities, in this case in the form of "cheap labor."

B. The Impact of Technology

The focus on the contributions of contemporary technology to commodity-consciousness necessitates an understanding of what is different now from the past. George Grant has pointed out in *Technology and Justice* that the very word *technology* provides an interesting point of departure for discussion. The word combines the Greek word *techne* ("art" or "craft" or "skill") with the Greek word *logos* ("science" or "knowledge" or "reason"). So, while we use the word to refer to the array of techniques or means by which we attain our desired ends, the word suggests, in Grant's words, a "co-penetration of art and science," a "co-penetration of knowing and making." This, in Grant's view, characterizes the contemporary technological mind-set and differentiates it from the simple production and use of tools for desired ends.

In other words, knowing and making are intertwined in contemporary consciousness in such a way that knowing is unto doing or making that will reveal new possibilities that, in turn, open up new forms of making. Technology is thus a whole way of thinking, not just a set of techniques. It is a way of thinking that regards what is to be known as a field of disposable energies. Martin Heidegger has said that our technological consciousness causes us to regard everything as "standing reserve." The world ceases to be a world of "objects" and becomes, more or less, a field of "possibilities."

To clarify by contrast, a non-technological and more contemplative mode of knowing might attempt simply to understand and appreciate. Such appreciative knowing was what Plato had in mind when he included science in his account of the ascent of eros, a form of knowing that would be an end in itself, rather than a means to the mastery of nature. Technological knowing, on the other hand, puts the will to mastery, which is the opposite of appreciation, at the heart of one's consciousness. The world to be known is not a world of actualities to be appreciated but a never-ending emergence of possibilities to be actualized.

If the meaning of contemporary technology is that our knowing is geared toward making (and that contemplation is more or less out the window), the question becomes, What do we want to make? If what people want to make is a less pain-filled, more comfortable, and more pleasurable existence, technology will be geared toward the production of a world of commodities. Technological consciousness and commodity-consciousness will kiss and embrace.

1. The Technological Imperative

But, more than this, technological consciousness brings something to this union that guarantees its fertility, the technological imperative. This imperative is to the effect that every "can" becomes an "ought" and then an "is." Since we *can* make an x, we *ought* to make an x. Therefore: *fiat* x. Further questions of value—ethical questions and questions of social policy—may be raised later, but for now the mere fact that we are able to expand our repertoire of techniques implies the value of doing so. And this, in turn, implies the value of producing whatever commodities the new techniques can produce, whether these be comfort-producing but ozone-depleting refrigerants, or fast-moving but air-polluting vehicles, or life-sustaining but coma-prolonging machines.

Given the technological imperative, the union of technological consciousness and commodity-consciousness cannot help but be prodigiously fertile. Any time a new commodity can be produced, it ought to be produce—at least for now. *Ad infinitum.* The problem with this is not simply that some of these commodities will bring with them unforeseen, bad side-effects, but also that a wrong-headed tendency will get reinforced, a tendency to look for fulfillment where fulfillment does not lie. An unbridled tendency to produce an endless string of commodities will not bring the desired fulfillment if something other than commodities is needed.

2. *The Computer Revisited*

Shifting the focus from technology in general to a particular area permits further exploration of the commoditizing possibilities present in the area of computer technology. First, as an advertising tool, the computer radiates commodity-consciousness. It should be added that as an expensive household item, it also symbolizes one of the effects of this consciousness, a widening gap between the haves and the have-nots, between those who have the latest, most complex information toys and those who do not.

Additionally, the computer opens up the possibility of storing and retrieving vast amounts of information about individual human beings. In the data banks that computers create and fill, there are clusters of information about human beings. Each person can easily become reduced to an information cluster that is accessible to the fingertips of a hacker or a detective or a representative of some business who might want to exercise some power. In this way, the computer creates and stores a commoditized version of each individual that can be and is bought and sold for a variety of purposes. If one is, for instance, the sort of person who might be interested in camping paraphernalia or excursions to gambling meccas, then one becomes susceptible to "personalized" advertising targeted to appeal to known interests. Is a person a good credit risk? Has a person ever been convicted of a crime or participated in a substance-abuse recovery program? Somewhere a computer data bank has the answer to these questions and, for a price, the information is retrievable by someone who will make a decision about an individual on the basis of the answer.

What is wrong with this? Should not sellers or employers or insurers or lenders or landlords and the like make informed decisions about the people they do business with? Why should the latest information technology not be put at the service of such informed decision making? These questions deserve a response.

Let it be granted that informed decisions are generally superior to uninformed decisions and that computer technology makes available a lot of information about individuals. Yet Alexander Pope's warning remains: "A little knowledge is a dangerous thing." Paradoxically, the megabytes of information that computers make available can easily add up to no more than "a little knowledge" when it comes to an individual person.

The problem is that, as a person, no one is a finished product, we are all in process. As individuals experience and think and feel and make decisions, they shape not only what is around them but also their very selves. People change, sometimes in small ways and sometimes in big ways. As a person who is in progress, someone may not necessarily like to be thought of as the person they no longer are. All the more, people may not want the incomplete version of what they once were in the past to represent what they are today.

But what is new about being misjudged? What is so new about people acting on the basis of incomplete or inaccurate information and, accordingly, treating other people unfairly? Put simply, the scale. For never before was it possible for so many people to be misunderstood and misjudged by so many other people at one time. And never before was it possible for so many people to act on the basis of what they "know" about others without those others having a clue about their being "known." Society is now dealing with an explosion of the possibilities for distortion, reductionism, and misjudgment.

To this quantitative problem is added, secondly, a qualitative dimension. The qualitative dimension has to do with the way computers are increasingly likely to be regarded, as if they are unassailable sources of the surest information available to human beings, as instruments of bedrock knowledge. The situation might be likened to the time when writing and a scriptoral culture gained a kind of ascendancy over speaking and oral culture. Later, the pitfalls as well as the benefits of the written word became clear.

If this analysis is correct, what does it mean? It does not mean that computers are bad and should not be used. It only means that this technology should not be idolized and should not be used indiscriminately. For computers are part of a commodity culture and, as such, they both nourish and are nourished by commodity-consciousness. And if this is not recognized, the use of computers will contribute to the commoditization and degradation of human beings.

V. ADDRESSING THE THREAT

How can society begin to address the threat that commodity-consciousness poses? Here it might be helpful to adopt something from the Buddhist tradition. When Siddhartha Gautama, the man who eventually came to be called the "Buddha" or "enlightened one," decided to offer his prescription for the transformation of human consciousness, he put forth an eight-part program that he called the "noble eightfold path." It is not the purpose of this chapter to elucidate either the Buddhist viewpoint in general or the Buddhist doctrine of the "eightfold path" in particular (see the chapter by James Dalton), but the first three parts of the eightfold path are particularly suggestive as a starting point to address the threat of commodity-consciousness. The Buddha pointed out that first one must have "right views" about the nature and causes of human suffering, and then one must have a "right attitude," which involves a resolute will to change what must be changed. He then spoke of a crucial way in which one begins to implement this will to change. He spoke of "right speech." The Buddha noted that the transformation of human consciousness requires the transformation of speech practices. In the present context, it can be suggested that the overcoming of commodity-consciousness by love-consciousness requires, as a starting point, right views, right attitude, and right speech.

A. Rights Views

To have "right views" is to come to full awareness of the presence and harmful influence of commodity-consciousness in one's culture and personal life. It is to be aware of the ways in which capitalism and contemporary technology contribute to the malaise of commodity-consciousness.

A voice that is both detached and prophetic is needed if as a people and as individuals we truly are to *see* where we are. It is especially encumbent upon those in educational and pastoral roles to provide this voice and to call attention to the ways in which commodity-consciousness infects our culture, working against both the upward ascent of eros and the outward reach of agape.

On Christmas night, 1996, a six-year-old girl, JonBenet Ramsey, was brutally murdered in her own home in Boulder, Colorado. Background news reports revealed that JonBenet was a child beauty-pageant queen, and scenes of her provocative singing and dancing flooded television for weeks. People rightly raised questions about the sexualization of children. But what did not seem to get noticed, and what a prophetic voice needed to make apparent, was that the sexualization of this little girl was not an aberration from, but only a poignant and tragic example of, the commodity culture we live in, a culture in which the presentation of oneself as an alluring commodity is something to be admired.

B. Right Attitude

To have a "right attitude" is to *will* to live counter to the pull of commodity-consciousness and to fight its effects on our culture. This includes a willingness to say no to capitalism as a *pure system* and to say yes to those aspects of the nation's mixed economy that hold the will to profit-making in check. It also includes a willingness to say no to the utopian idealization of technology and to the technological imperative as such. Not every *can* merits a transformation into an *ought*. This means saying yes to ethics committees and public policy think tanks that would examine the ethical and social implications of new technological possibilities, notably in the area of information technology, *before* these are actuated and have gathered inertial force.

Those in educational and pastoral roles can make a special contribution to the cultivation of right attitude. They can become signs of contradiction with regard to commodity-consciousness. This applies to institutions as well as to individuals. It requires living against the grain and sometimes letting go of "the bottom line" and evincing faith. For instance, employment decisions can be made with an eye to a kind of justice that goes beyond a corporate concern for efficiency and economy. When churches and church-affiliated schools are not recognizably different in their employment practices from business corporations, the opportunity for a sign of contradiction has been lost. Commodity-consciousness is lodged more deeply and securely in the national mind as a result.

C. Right Speech

The nature and importance of "right speech," in the present context, merits a bit more extended treatment. Our language does not merely express whatever we may consciously and deliberately intend but also underlying patterns of thinking that belong to us as individuals and as participants in a particular culture or subculture. Our linguistic expression of these thought patterns, in turn, reinforces them. It thus becomes crucial at times to change our language if we are to change our own or our culture's thought patterns.

Just as the rooting out of sexism from our culture requires (as a necessary though by no means sufficient condition) the rooting out of sexist language from our speech practices, so something similar must be done with regard to language that betrays and reinforces the presence of commodity-consciousness.

What are some examples of commoditizing language? Consider first the seemingly innocent words "employer" and "employee," words that are so much a part of capitalist culture. To employ means to use; to be employed is to be used. An employer is one who uses another human being and thus controls him or her. An employee is one who is used and controlled by another. The innocence of the usage is taken for granted, yet the usage betrays an underlying thought pattern that is destructive because it involves thinking of human beings as commodities. This is no more unreasonable than saying that the use of the word *man* to refer to the whole human race involves a put-down of women.

A second example, connected with the first, is the use of the word *personnel* to describe the body of persons that a particular organization makes use of. It is not too difficult to pick up on the commoditizing tone of this word, especially when it is used as a parallel to the word *materiel*. Perhaps for this reason many "personnel" offices have become departments of "human resources." (Unfortunately, the phrase can convey the idea that human beings are resources to be used, which would be another instance of commoditizing language. As a matter of historical fact, however, the term is more aligned with a movement in management theory that concerns itself with empowering workers; the phrase refers not to the workers themselves but to the resources they bring with them.)

Examples of commoditizing language can be multiplied. We speak of the "worth" of a person in terms of dollars: "My net worth is about five million dollars." We refer to an athlete who is about to turn professional as a "product" of a certain university. In the world of professional sports, we talk every day, innocently and casually, about people being "traded" or "sold."

The attempt to develop "right speech" would not, of itself, be sufficient to transport our culture and ourselves from commodity-consciousness. It is a beginning and not a conclusion. Still remaining would be the essential work to overhaul other practices that were exposed by changing linguistic practices. Replacing the terms *employee* and *employer* would be futile if the pertinent relations did not change for the better. But the effort to transform language would at least exert a pull in the direction of further transformation.

These steps can go a long way toward lessening the threat to human dignity that is posed by our modern culture.

It will take time. But the ancient Chinese proverb remains true: *A journey of a thousand miles begins beneath one's own feet.*

REFERENCES

Aristotle. *Nichomachean Ethics.* Tr. Terrence Irwin. Indianapolis: Hacket Publishing Company, 1985.

Descartes, René. *Meditations on First Philosophy.* Tr. John Cottingham. Cambridge: Cambridge University Press, 1986.

Grant, George. *Technology and Justice.* Notre Dame, Ind.: University of Notre Dame Press, 1986.

Heidegger, Martin. "The Question of Technology," in *Basic Writings from Being in Time to the Task of Thinking.* Ed. David Farrell Krell. New York: Harper & Row, 1977.

Illych, Ivan. Lecture given at Univerity of Denver, 1975.

Kant, Immanuel. *Groundwork of the Metaphysic of Morals.* Tr. H. J. Paton. New York: Harper Torchbooks, 1964.

Plato. *Symposium.* Tr. Robin Waterfield. Oxford: Oxford University Press, 1994.

Wordsworth, William. "The World Is Too Much with Us." *The Norton Anthology of Poetry.* New York: W. W. Norton & Company, 1975.

Preaching about Dignity or Preaching with Dignity

Edward Foley, Capuchin

Sunday held little promise of relief from the six-day heat wave. By the time 11:00 mass began at St. Timothy's, it was clear that the rising temperature and oppressive humidity would render the normally stoic congregation more listless than usual. The entrance rites and readings were quickly dispatched without much passion, but also with little complaint from the assembly. As the fans were temporarily silenced and the congregation sat in quiet resignation for the homily, however, they knew that neither season, temperature, nor dew-point reading would have any influence on the length or quality of Monsignor Carter's sermon.

The gospel from the end of the thirteenth chapter of Matthew was a mystery to most worshipers, but Monsignor Carter was going to explain it to them. A brief excursus on the nature of parable soon gave way to a moralistic exposition of each of the three parables in the passage. For twenty-seven minutes the preacher explained to them that the great hidden treasure for them was their faith; that the pearl was the church, and that mass was like a net thrown into the sea, catching fish of every kind. "But just coming to mass is not going to save you," he chided, "because as the gospel says, when the net was brought to shore, the disciples picked through the fish, saving the good and throwing out the bad. So will you be judged, says the gospel, separated into evil and righteous by the angels at the last judgment. You know what you have to do to avoid condemnation: you adults stop sinning, children respect your parents, everyone pray the rosary, and be more faithful about coming to mass. Maybe then, through God's mercy, you can hope to find yourself standing with the righteous at the last judgment. In the name of the Father, and of the Son...." The monsignor's voice trailed off and the fans were restarted. As a slight breeze filled the air an almost audible sigh of relief rose from the assembly, grateful for this modicum of relief from what could only be considered a stifling environment.

It is not a great revelation to Christians in general, or Roman Catholics in particular, that the preaching in our worship is a mixed blessing. Sometimes it is unquestionably splendid, an authentic experience of grace and revelation. More frequently, however, it is mediocre, and on some occasions it devolves to the level of tedium or oppression.[1]

Even where the preaching receives a generally positive response, a common complaint is that it is often in danger of descending into the boring or irrelevant (Sweetser and Forster, 1993, 17–18). It is possible that such a complaint is simply the cry of easily distracted, television-bred worshipers who would happily trade their pew for a comfortable chair and the missalette or hymnal in their hand for their beloved remote control. The underlying concern of such malcontents, as summarized by noted television critic Neil Postman, could simply be a yearning to be entertained. According to Postman, television has not only presented us with entertaining subject matter, but it presents all subject matter as entertaining (Postman, 1985, 87). Thus politics, education, and even religion as transmitted via television are perceived as distinctive but related forms of entertainment. The cumulative impact of this experience is that—even apart from television—we expect all experiences of politics, education, and religion to be entertaining. In worship this can manifest itself as a desire for presiders and preachers who are more like Jerry Seinfeld or Jay Leno than St. Timothy's Monsignor Carter.

There is little doubt that the television-bred expectation to be entertained influences the contemporary assessment of liturgical preaching.[2] Yet, the concern about liturgical preaching as boring or irrelevant is not wholly a matter of communication techniques or audience satisfaction. It is also, at its core, profoundly theological and raises significant questions about the dignity of individual hearers and assemblies of believers. To weigh the responses and expectations of an assembly in the preaching act is, in fact, to address the ecclesial status of the assembly. Ultimately, to consider the experiences and needs of ordinary believers in the preaching event is to ponder whether they are simply the *objects* of this liturgical ministry—and, by consequence, objects of the theological opinions and ecclesial decisions that support and direct such ministry—or whether, in a true sense, they are authentic and primary *subjects* of the same.

I. LITURGY AS REHEARSAL OF HUMAN DIGNITY

The whole of this volume addresses issues of human dignity. The focus on preaching in the liturgical assembly for Roman Catholics is a particular case study within that wider topic. It is possible that a consideration of the preaching event might appear to be a somewhat introspective case study with few implications about the dignity of human beings outside the worshiping event, or even outside the church which internally prescribes and regulates such worship. The presupposition of this author, however, is that the liturgical preaching event is not simply one topic among many that suggests itself for consideration under the rubric of human dignity. Rather, liturgical preaching as a pivotal moment in the church's official worship is a critical, self-defining activity in which the church publicly models and rehearses what it genuinely believes about the dignity of the baptized and, by implication, the dignity of other human beings as well.

The Judaeo-Christian tradition teaches that revelation is fundamentally an auditory-dynamic event (Foley, 1996, chap. 1). More specifically, Christian revelation teaches that faith comes through hearing the preached word (Rom 10:14). Thus preaching is "the essential means by which the Church communicates the gospel of Jesus Christ" (Burke and Doyle, 1986, 40). While preaching assumes a variety of different forms and occurs in diverse contexts, it has a particular and integral relationship to the church's official worship (Constitution on the Sacred Liturgy, hereafter CSL, §52). As defined by the Second Vatican Council, the whole of the church's life is anticipated and epitomized in the liturgy, which is recognized as the summit and fount of our life (§10). Thus one could consider our public worship—and the constitutive elements of that worship such as preaching—a rehearsal of our life in Christ.

Liturgy authentically understood and lived is not an empty statement about a distant God or a ritualized dream about idealized human
relationships. Rather, it is a symbolic activity: what the U.S. bishops in
their statement "Music in Catholic Worship" call "vehicles of communication and instruments of faith" (§7). From this perspective, the act of
public worship has both an expressive and creative quality—a past and a
future—for it both reflects what is already lived and believed while
simultaneously calling forth a new faith and lived integrity with that
belief. Worship faithfully celebrated, therefore, has the potential to create the reality it signifies. Thus it is possible to imagine liturgy as a
"rehearsal" of the Christian life. Rehearsal, in this sense, is not simply a
dramatic enactment of some long-finished historical event. Nor is it an
imperfect repetition of some act in order to get it right. Rather, rehearsal
so conceived is a continual reentry into and further appropriation of a
dynamic and inexhaustible reality that has profound ramifications
beyond the immediate experience of the symbolic event. Rehearsal so
imagined is neither artificial nor preparatory; it is rather ritual engagement with the truth in a symbolic mode which provides real agency for
such truth. Participation in the church's liturgy, therefore, is a cardinal
rehearsal of the Christian vocation: reiterating our call in faith and fore-
shadowing our response in Christ.

This perspective requires that we not only consider liturgical
preaching from the viewpoint of its hoped-for effect after the event, but
also to consider the nature of its modeling within worship, since these
two aspects of preaching are intimately linked. Preaching not only articulates what we are supposed to do or who we are to become, but like the
rest of the liturgy, it also announces by virtue of the liturgical act itself
who we are. From the viewpoint of human dignity, therefore, one can
ask: does the preaching event simply call people to dignity, or does it
actually model and rehearse the dignity of the assembly in the process?
Is the preaching event only about the insights, feelings, and ministry of
the preacher, or is it also about the insights, feelings, and ministry of the
assembly? Does the preacher and preaching event symbolically proclaim the assembly to be the object of the preaching event—and by
implication the object of the liturgy and the object of the church's ministry—or does it symbolically assert that the assembly is more properly
understood to be the subject of such preaching? To the extent that former
occurs, then to that same extent is the baptismal dignity of the assembly

of believers demeaned and, by extension, is the dignity of all those whom the church would treat as "objects" of preaching and ministry demeaned. To the extent, however, that the assembly is endorsed and embraced as subject of preaching, worship, and ministry, so is their dignity rehearsed, affirmed, and anticipated even in those who have not nor never will accept the gospel of Jesus Christ.

A. Realigning Priorities

Accepting liturgical preaching as a symbolic rehearsal of human dignity may require not only a readjustment of one's definition of a homily, but also a reconsideration of basic presuppositions about the nature and purpose of this particular genre of preaching. While focused specifically on the eucharistic homily, John Burke and Thomas Doyle outline a number of misconceptions that are generally true of all forms of liturgical preaching (Burke and Doyle, 1986, 235). Many, for example, believe that the essential component of the homily is an exegesis of the day's scriptural reading(s), while others who might consider themselves more "liturgical" assume that such preaching must explain the nature of the feast, the sacramental rite being celebrated, or the liturgical "theme" of the day. Those with a systematic bent might hold that liturgical preaching is a didactic moment appropriate for providing some instruction on a favorite or neglected doctrinal subject, while others take this as an opportunity for moral exhortation to Christian behavior. Finally, the homily is occasionally transformed into an appeal for money, a pitch for volunteers to help with the parish carnival, or a means for further engaging the worshipers in some other aspect of the parish's life.

The paradox is that while none of these images of liturgical preaching is exactly on target, each makes a valid yet ancillary point about the homiletic event. For example, while liturgical preaching is not essentially an exegetical nor liturgical exposition, it should be grounded in a credible interpretation of the day's scripture readings and the liturgical feast or rite being celebrated. Similarly, though liturgical preaching is first of all neither an opportunity for teaching basic tenets of faith nor for moral exhortation, it should be doctrinally sound and underscore the ethical implications of Christian living. Even the homily turned financial appeal or recruitment seminar points to the need for liturgical preaching to engage worshipers in the building up of the local community of faith.

If at its heart, however, liturgical preaching is neither exegesis, explanation, instruction, exhortation, nor recruitment ploy, then what is it? The beginning of an answer to that sometimes perplexing question is found in the crucial modifier that distinguishes this type of preaching from all others,[3] namely liturgical. Since, as noted above, the homily is integrally related to the liturgy, and it is the liturgy to which the church gives pride of place as fount and summit of ecclesial life, then it is to the liturgy that one must look for an appropriate definition of liturgical preaching.

In its exposition on the nature of the liturgy, the CSL notes a number of critical elements about the official public worship of the church. Therein we learn that the liturgy is a celebration of the central mystery of the death and resurrection of Christ (§6); is a way to give thanks to God for the inexpressible gift in Christ Jesus through the power of the Holy Spirit (§6); is an action of Christ the Priest and of his body the church (§7); is an experience of presence (§7); is a fundamental source of the church's spiritual life (§§12, 13); and presumes the full, conscious, and active participation of all the baptized, which is both their right and their responsibility (§14). In a summary way, the CSL notes that the "liturgy is the source for achieving in the most effective way possible human sanctification and God's glorification" (§10).

Attempting to define liturgical preaching within this larger frame of the nature of the liturgy provides some useful correctives to the misconceptions about the homily noted above. It also provides a firm direction for shaping preaching as authentically liturgical, an appropriate rehearsal of the dignity of the baptized, and an implicit affirmation of the dignity of all human beings. It suggests, for example, that liturgical preaching is less exegesis or instruction than it is proclamation, and that proclamation is of a person rather than an idea. The focus on Christ, and the language of presence and action in CSL's discussion of the nature of liturgy, suggests that liturgical preaching, like the liturgy itself, is meant to be a privileged and transformative encounter with God through Christ in the Spirit.

II. THE TURN TOWARD THE ASSEMBLY

What may be surprising to the preacher who reflects on the nature of the liturgy according to CSL is that the transformative encounter that preaching enables is not essentially an encounter between the preacher and the congregation, but between the latter and God! As well noted in "Fulfilled in Your Hearing" (hereafter FIYH), a statement of the U.S. Bishops' Committee on Priestly Life and Ministry, the homilist has an important mediating role in this encounter. The preacher represents the community "by voicing its concerns, by naming its demons, and thus enabling it to gain some understanding and control of the level which afflicts it. [The preacher] represents the Lord by offering the community another word, a word of healing and pardon, of acceptance and love" (§13).⁴ Yet this mediation role precisely underscores that, as in worship, the two critical parties in the preaching encounter are God and the church, God and the assembly.

Such an awareness makes the point that it is not only the preacher who has some responsibilities here, but also the assembly. If the assembly is one of two essential parties in the ritual conversation called preaching, they need to be engaged. Preparation is an important task for members of the assembly: both remote preparation for hearing the word that takes place even before one arrives for worship as well as immediate preparation during the liturgy itself, for example, by careful listening to the proclamation of the readings. Furthermore, members of the assembly need to cultivate a spirit of reflective openness in the preaching event, where they must practice attentiveness, even vulnerability to the Word which not only calms and consoles, but challenges and confronts as well.

While the assembly has mighty responsibilities in this ritual conversation called preaching, those responsibilities are often more individual than communal. It is the presider and preacher, on the other hand, who have a critical and determinative responsibility for setting the public ethos that can enable a spirit of openness and vulnerability required of the assembly in the preaching event. As the U.S. Bishops' Committee on the Liturgy noted in "Music in Catholic Worship," no single factor affects worship as much as the attitude, style, and bearing of the presider (§21). We would contend that the same is true of the preacher. Thus, without denying the responsibilities of the assembly in the preaching event, this article will focus on the responsibilities of preachers, particularly in their call to facilitate the ritual conversation between God and the assembly.

FIYH underscores the preacher's responsibility to attend carefully to the worshiping community by beginning its discussion of "The Homily in the Sunday Assembly" (the subtitle of the work) with the *assembly*. FIYH comments that beginning the treatment of the Sunday homily with the assembly rather than the preacher is not only appropriate but actually essential (§4). The reasons for this, according to FIYH, are twofold. First, from the viewpoint of communication theory, the document stresses that an accurate understanding of the audience is necessary if communication is to be effective.

> Unless a preacher knows what a congregation needs, wants, or is able to hear, there is every possibility that the message offered in the homily will not meet the needs of the people who hear it. To say this is by no means to imply that preachers are only to preach what their congregations want to hear. Only when preachers know what their congregations want to hear will they be able to communicate what a congregation needs to hear. Homilists may indeed preach on what they understand to be the real issues, but if they are not in touch with what the people think are the real issues, they will very likely be misunderstood or not heard at all. What is communicated is not what is said, but it is what is heard, and what is heard is determined in large measure by what the hearer needs or wants to hear. (§4)

Even more telling, however, is the second reason, which FIYH considers more fundamental, and that reason is ecclesiological.

> The Dogmatic Constitution on the Church describes the church as the mystery of God's saving will, given concrete historical expression in the people with whom he has entered into a covenant. This church is the visible sacrament of the saving union to which God calls all people....The church, therefore, is first and foremost a gathering of those whom the Lord has called into a covenant of peace with himself. In this gathering, as in every other, offices and ministries are necessary, but secondary. The primary reality is Christ in the assembly, the People of God. (§5)

It is this ecclesiological position, rather than any insight derived from communication theory, that is at the basis of the assertion that liturgical preaching is an event in which the church, in a pivotal way, rehearses the human dignity of the baptized and the dignity of the whole human family as well. It is also the basis for understanding that the transformative encounter that liturgical preaching is supposed to enable is fundamentally an encounter between believers and God, not between the assembly and the preacher.

A. The Dignity of the Baptized

The value of believers does not flow from the nature of the ministry directed toward them nor the quality of the ministers who care for them. It is not contingent upon some other human being, such as a homilist. Rather, according to the Dogmatic Constitution of the Church, the dignity of the baptized flows from their divine call, their rebirth in Christ, and their vocation to perfection (§32). All the baptized are called by God to intimacy with God (§§39ff) and it is this intimacy, this transformative union that the homilist must enable. In so doing, the liturgical preacher fulfills his or her proper function as a "mediator of meaning" (FIYH §12), enabling the divinely initiated dialogue between God and the assembly of believers to grow ever more strongly.

This ecclesiological assertion of the dignity of the baptized, apart from any human agency, as rehearsed within the official liturgy of the church mirrors the dignity of all human beings who participate in what Karl Rahner calls the liturgy of the world. The Roman Catholic Church teaches that the "plan of salvation" includes not only the Catholic faithful and all Christians, but also Jews, Muslims, and all those who sincerely seek God (Dogmatic Constitution on the Church §§14–16). Not only does the church teach that all such people are called to salvation, but also that they are gifted by God with grace to live a good life (§16).

Rahner explains this gift of grace in terms of God's self-communication which is not limited to the baptized, nor somehow dispensed within the confines of particular ritual or devotional activities. Rather, God's self-communication and call to salvation occurs throughout the whole of human history.

> ...the freedom of acceptance or refusal of salvation occurs in all the dimensions of human existence, and it occurs always in an encounter with the world and not merely in the confined sector of the sacred or of worship and "religion" in the narrow sense, it occurs in encounters with one's neighbor,

with one's historical task, with the so-called world of every-
day life, in and with what we call the history of the individual
and of communities. Thus salvation-history takes place right
in the midst of ordinary history. (Rahner, 1983, 98–99)

Rahner believes that the world is permeated by the grace of God, constantly
and ceaselessly possessed by God's self-communication from its innermost roots (Rahner, 1976, 166). This continuous self-communication of
God through all of human history is what Rahner calls the liturgy of the
world. "The world and its history are the terrible and sublime liturgy,
breathing of death and sacrifice, which God celebrates and causes to be celebrated in and through human history in its freedom, this being something
which he in turn sustains in grace by his sovereign disposition" (Rahner,
1976, 169).

It is this liturgy, according to Rahner, that is fundamental and prior
to any particular notion of ecclesial worship. It is the liturgy of the world
that unequivocally demonstrates that true worship is not so much the
enactment of rubrics as it is what happens when "we freely immerse
ourselves in the abiding, absolute mystery during the great and small
moments of life" (Skelley, 1991, 93–94). What occurs in the particular
and defined sacramental action of the church that we call liturgy is,
according to Rahner, a symbolic manifestation of the liturgy of the
world. It is where the church enacts in sign and symbol its "concrete
self-fulfillment...as the basic sacrament of salvation for the world"
(Rahner, 1976, 181). Michael Skelley elaborates:

When we participate in the Church's liturgy, we are not
doing something basically different from other activities but
explicitly focusing on the deepest meaning of those activities. The liturgy of the Church is the explicit manifestation
of the implicit liturgy of our lives. It is not simply identical
with that liturgy of the world, but it is so derived from it and
deeply united with it that it really expresses the cosmic
liturgy and makes it present to us. (Skelley, 1991, 101)

Specifically addressing the act of liturgical preaching in this context
suggests not only that the manner of such preaching rehearses the dignity
of the baptized assembly participating in the liturgy, but also by implication rehearses the dignity of the human family enmeshed in the liturgy of

the world. Engaging the assembly in a transformational encounter with the divine in the preaching act, treating them not as objects but as subjects in the divine-human dialogue, and attending to their needs in the facilitation of such an encounter is a symbolic rehearsal of the respect due to all human beings. Conversely, treating a liturgical assembly as a captive audience of the homilist's personal whim or lecturing them as though a group of wayward children or spiritual neophytes rehearses a similar contempt for others outside ecclesial boundaries. Quite frankly, if homilists are incapable of recognizing and upholding the dignity of the baptized in the church's official worship where we bathe, chrismate, robe, and feed them with the body of Christ, it is difficult to imagine that such respect will be extended to those outside of this royal people.

B. Validating Experience, Engaging Praxis

Acknowledging that the preaching act is a critical, self-defining activity in which the church publicly models and rehearses what it genuinely believes about the dignity of the baptized and, by implication, the dignity of all human beings is a critical step that each homilist must take. Beyond cognitive assent to this insight, however, preachers need to reckon, in action, with its consequences. While there are many ways this might be accomplished, few are more important than admitting the real experiences of worshipers as determinative for the preaching paradigm in particular, and the practice of ministry in general.

This turn toward people's real experience is already acknowledged in the previously cited FIYH. Therein the U.S. bishops recognize that people who gather for worship come with very particular questions:

> How [can] this God, whom the Scriptures present as so powerful and so loving, be experienced in lives today that seem so broken and meaningless? How can parents believe in a God who raises the dead to life when their daughter has just been killed in a car accident? How can a family hope in a god who leads his people out of slavery into freedom when they are trapped in an inflationary spiral in which costs increase and the buying power of their salaries diminishes? How can young people join with the angels and saints in praise of the glory of God when they are struggling with the

challenges of establishing their own identities and their relationship to family and friends? (§12)

The need for preachers to attend to such questions and experiences is not just for the sake of more effective communication, larger crowds, or high approval ratings. Rather, it is imperative that these ministers proclaim the Word in such a way that respects people's questions and validates their experiences because these questions and experiences are at the core of our definition of church and are driving fundamental changes in contemporary Roman Catholic theology.

As previously noted, FIYH argues for the assembly as the beginning point for any consideration of liturgical preaching because of the ecclesiological presupposition that the assembly is the church. While this is a welcomed and critical development, it is also insufficient for an adequate theology of preaching, especially when such is considered as a rehearsal of human dignity. It is insufficient, because while it is critical to begin with the assembly in developing an adequate theology of preaching, it is also necessary to ask further "the assembly according to whom?" It is possible—some might argue even traditional in some strands of Roman Catholicism—to offer ecclesiological definitions of and shape practice for the laity without ever having sought their input or mined their experiences in the shaping of such definitions and practice. The result has often been the emergence of theological opinion, doctrinal positions, and subsequent ministerial activity that is often quite out of touch with people's lived experiences.

While there are many examples of this lack of attention to an assembly's real experiences in shaping a theology and practice for preaching and worship, some of the most poignant occur with marginalized people, such as those with developmental disabilities.

> Four special education groups had been meeting for some time in a small parish in a large city before it became clear that no one in any of those groups had been confirmed. The pastor and parents agreed on a date in May one year later when they would request the presence of the bishop for the sacrament....As the plans for the liturgy developed the pastor of the parish made several unsuccessful efforts to contact the office of the bishop in order to clarify some special, simplifying aspects of the liturgy that had been planned. A request was

made that the bishop come early to meet the members of the group. He was encouraged to proceed slowly with the process of confirming so that each candidate could approach with his or her family with a minimum of confusion when their names were called....

The bishop arrived just in time for the celebration. He seemed uncomfortable with the people who had gathered and impatient with the pace of the service. His homily was addressed to the parents and encouraged them to bear the cross God gave them with such children. During the confirmation itself, he seemed pressed for time and therefore created a minor traffic problem by trying to hurry things along. The bishop rejected the presentation of the bread baked by one of the groups and sent the just-ordained master of ceremonies to the sacristy for a large white host. The bishop communicated by taking the white host and then sat down. The various priests involved in the program gave communion to the disabled. The bishop instructed the priests to put all the bread into their mouths even if they put their hands out to receive. (Foley, 1994, 86–87)

It is one thing to begin defining an assembly according to some preconceived notions or theologies. It is quite another thing to begin that definitional work in view of an assembly's real experiences. The former renders them objects of worship and preaching, once again, while the latter is a necessary move in enabling them to become authentic subjects of worship and preaching. People with developmental disabilities, like other human beings, have valid experiences. Furthermore, in Rahner's terms, the self-communication of God is mediated through such experiences. They, too, share in the awesome liturgy of the world. How revelatory and challenging it becomes when their experiences of the liturgy of the world and their perceptions of the God who sustains the world's liturgy begin to invade, shape, and even permeate the worship in our churches.

C. The Significance of Human Experience

This need to acknowledge ordinary human experience as a valid, even requisite consideration in the preparation and enactment of liturgical preaching is related to a wider movement in theology and ministry today that asserts again the critical significance of human experience in these ventures. One prominent articulation of this move is found in the methodological classic by James and Evelyn Whitehead, *Method in Ministry.* In this work on theological reflection and Christian ministry,[5] the Whiteheads present a tri-partite model that points to three sources of religiously significant information to be brought to bear on pastoral decisions: Christian tradition, personal experience, and culture. Experience in this model refers to that set of ideas, feelings, biases, and insights that a particular minister and community bring to a pastoral reflection for the shaping of Christian practice (Whitehead, 1995, 53). It is the conviction of the Whiteheads and others that particular human experience is so critical for the shaping of ministry and theology that theological reflection should begin here (Whitehead, 1995, 17). Indeed, the past decade has witnessed the reshaping of an entire theological discipline known as practical theology, which in many respects is built upon the affirmation of the primacy of human experience for theology (Browning, 1991, 9 and passim).

Proponents of practical theology are symbolic of broad developments in academic theology that wish to reassert the practical nature of theology itself (Maddox, 1990) and its necessary reliance on human experience and communal praxis.[6] Human experience is recognized as laden with the theory that systematic theology articulates, but such theory is always for the purpose of practice. Theological paradigms and ministerial practice that take human experience seriously thus suggest what has been characterized as a practice-theory-practice dynamic. This is quite different from a theory-practice paradigm that begins with the articulation of a priori ministerial or theological principles, which, in turn, direct and inform pastoral application but are not necessarily influenced by the same (Tracy, 1983, 61). In liturgical and sacramental theology this broad movement toward the reintegration of praxis into the theological paradigm is reflected in the turn from metaphysical to anthropological categories, and the preference for "relationship" rather than agency or causality as the primary category for exploring human and divine interaction (Schillebeeckx, 1968, 107–121).

Liturgical preaching that does not seriously consider the experiences of the liturgical assembly in its preparation, enactment, and critique is preaching trapped in a theory-practice paradigm. Such preaching may attempt or even desire that the assembly be subject and not simply object in the preaching act, but such good intentions are insufficient if they do not reckon with real community praxis—and not simply the preacher's assessment of community praxis–as self-definitional for the preaching act. The experience of the assembly is the foundational, theory-laden praxis that must be mined in the preaching process. It is the real world experience of the assembly that provides a particular manifestation of the liturgy of the world and God's self-communication that must be determinative for its symbolic manifestation in the church's official liturgy. And it is the real world experience of the assembly that must be publicly rehearsed in the preaching event so that the preaching event, in turn, may rehearse the dignity of the assembly, which in itself is a symbolic manifestation of the dignity of all human beings.

III. A STRATEGY FOR PREACHING WITH DIGNITY

There are a number of things that a homilist can do that will contribute to the validation of people's real experiences in the preaching act, engage them as subjects in the divine-human dialogue, symbolically rehearse their dignity, and by extension rehearse the dignity of others in the homiletic event. Fred Baumer suggests, for example, that much of this can be achieved by employing what he calls transactional rather than transmissive speech. According to Baumer, the transmissive speech is a type of language used to deliver ready-made truths, whereas transactional speech engages people as subjects rather than as objects of preaching, enabling them to discern meaning rather than receive truth (Baumer, 1985, chap. 6). Baumer's emphasis on transactional language finds much resonance in FIYH,[7] which suggests that the homily should have the tone of a personal conversation (§63), might begin with addressing the human situation rather than interpreting scriptural texts (§65), and should employ specific, graphic and imaginative language that invites people to respond from the heart as well as from the mind (§67).

An even more radical strategy for engaging the assembly as subjects of the preaching act is the largely unheeded suggestion by FIYH to involve members of the congregation directly in the preparation of the homily through what the document calls a "homily preparation group." As envisioned by FIYH, this group would consist of four or five members of the congregation, with one member of the group dropping out and another being added every four weeks or so (§106). The primary responsibility of the group would be to gather with the homilist at the beginning of the week and reflect on the appointed scriptures for the coming Sunday.[8] Such a group of ordinary parishioners would have a very different purpose than, for example, some gathering of priests or members of a parish staff. While groups exclusively comprised of the latter may be a rich resource of insight, it is the presence of members from the assembly according to FIYH that are "especially helpful in raising issues that are of concern to them and which the homily may be able to address" (§107).

The idea of a homily preparation group is somewhat underdeveloped in FIYH and could appear as a pleasant but wholly peripheral afterthought to the document. This is unfortunate, for it is difficult to imagine any other mode of homily preparation that could help to ensure that the homilist reckons with real experiences of the assembly, and further ensures that the assembly is consistently respected as subject in the homiletic discourse. While it is true that the random interaction of the preacher with members of the assembly during the week is important for homily preparation, and can profoundly influence that preparation, this is no substitute for explicit and systematic engagement with members of the assembly about the preaching event.[9]

There is also no substitute for systematic feedback and evaluation of the preaching from this group. One other underdeveloped aspect of FIYH is its lack of attention to such critique in the context of the homily preparation group. While FIYH does note that evaluation is a nonnegotiable element of effective preaching (§111), the document does not explicate any clear context for such critique. Who better to provide ongoing feedback to the homilist, however, than the group that shared in the shaping of the homily in the first place? The expectation for regular feedback from members of the congregation through a homily preparation group, and the processing of such feedback is not first of all a means to monitor the homilist in the fulfillment of her or his responsibility to the assembly, but more so is a crucial way for the assembly through its representatives to assert their responsibility for the homiletic act.

It is possible that this ongoing engagement, preparation, and critique between homilist and members of the assembly might be a source of anxiety or even frustration for the homilist. While every attempt should be made to avoid frustrating homilists, or thwarting their sincere efforts to preach the Word, the comfort of the minister is not the essential concern in this enterprise. Rather, it is the proper enactment of the liturgical preaching event, so that the Word is appropriately broken open for the community, and the community is empowered to make a genuine response to that Word.

An ancient Christian maxim teaches that the public worship of the church is foundational for the church's belief: *lex orandi, lex credendi.*[10] Given the symbolic role Christian worship plays not only in shaping faith, but also acknowledging the worth of those whose faith are shaped in the liturgical act, it seems also important to assert the principle of *lex orandi, lex dignandi.*[11] The church's liturgy is a treasured event in which our salvation is announced and our identity is rehearsed. And so it is there we discover not only that it is right and just *(dignum et justum est)* to give God thanks and praise, but it is also right and just to assert the dignity of the assembly which, in the words of Eucharistic Prayer II, has been "found worthy to stand in God's presence and serve...."

Those who preach the Word are charged with an awesome responsibility. They are commissioned to proclaim Good News, and articulate the sacramental presence of God in the proclaimed Word (CSL §7). In doing so, however, they are also responsible for rendering the preaching event itself as good news, an encounter in grace, and an affirmation of the dignity of those who encounter the Word in the church's liturgy and the liturgy of the world. When that occurs, especially by sustained and respectful affirmation of the communal praxis which is the crucible for that Word, then the true purpose of the homiletic event has been achieved in the glorification of God and the sanctification of people.

> Quite frankly, Linda couldn't have told you anything about the just proclaimed gospel as she sat down for the sermon. She had been distracted by her restless four-year-old son, and the fact that she had no idea what she was going to fix for her in-laws who were coming over for dinner that evening. She was in the midst of a mental inventory of her pantry when Fr. Zachary, the pastor, broke in with the opening line of his sermon. "Hello, Salt." He bellowed. The community chuckled, and Linda remembered, "Oh yes, 'salt of the earth' gospel."
>
> "You are the salt of the earth," he said. "You are the fizz in a Coke, the snap in a rubber band, the pop in Orville

Redenbacker's popcorn. But what if the Coke is flat? It is tasteless, and is quickly dumped down the drain. And what if the rubber band has no snap? That too is worthless, and needs to be thrown away. And what if popcorn doesn't pop? Then it's inedible...and all those burned kernels need to be dumped in the garbage." Linda had no idea where he was going, but Fr. Zach certainly had her attention. Her husband calls her a popcorn addict, and she hates it when the stuff doesn't pop.

"And what about you?" he asked. "You are not Coke, or a rubber band, or popcorn...but you are Christian: baptized, most of you confirmed, people who Sunday after Sunday come to the table and receive the Body of Christ. And if Coke is suppose to fizz, and rubber bands are suppose to snap and popcorn is suppose to pop, then aren't you...aren't WE to be Christian, to be the Body of Christ in the world?" Linda shifted uncomfortably in her pew. She did go to communion every week, like she was taught, but didn't think much about being the body of Christ. How was she suppose to be Christ's body?

"In Matthew's gospel, Jesus challenges us to be salt and light: to be the incarnation of the Good News in the world today," Fr. Zach continued. "It is not just the women religious, or the parish staff, or your HOLY pastor," Linda smirked, "who is responsible for witnessing the presence of Christ in the world. This is something for which all of us are responsible. But how do we do that? How do we become salt and light and Body in our lives?" Linda wasn't sure how to answer.

Fr. Zach continued, "There is no one answer to that question, but maybe we find some direction in the story of the old Rabbi." Linda really enjoyed Fr. Zach's stories, even though he sometimes repeated them. She didn't think that she had heard this one before, however. "It seems that the Rabbi asked his students how they could tell when the night had ended and the day was on its way. 'Could it be,' asked one, 'when you can see an animal in the distance and can tell whether it is a sheep or a dog?' 'No,' said the rabbi. 'Is it,' asked another, 'when you can look at a distant tree and tell whether it is an olive or a fig?' 'No,' said the rabbi. 'Is it,' asked a third, 'when you can gaze into a cup and tell whether the liquid is water or wine?' 'No,' said the rabbi. 'Then tell us,' they demanded, 'tell us when you know that the night has ended and the day is on its way.' 'It is,' said the rabbi, 'when you can look into the face of any woman or man and see that they are your sister or brother, because if you cannot do this then it is still night no matter what the time.'"

Fr. Zach continued, "We live in a world with many shadows. We know a lot of people who live in darkness: who feel alone, unloved, rejected." Linda thought of her mother-in-law coming over for dinner that night. Here was a woman who lived under a cloud. "Sometimes we are the source of their shadows. Jesus charges us, however, not to be shadow-casters, or light-extinguishers, but to be luminous, shining witnesses of God's presence—Christ's Body in the world." Linda knew that her mother-in-law enjoyed her time with her son and only grandson; it was always a bright spot in her life. Linda just didn't have much energy or enthusiasm for her visits. "We cannot let the darkness continue and still call ourselves Christian. Even more, we cannot be a source of shadows or despair or rejection for others and still proclaim ourselves to be the baptized, the enlightened ones, the witnesses of Christ to the world." Linda swallowed hard.

"We come here to refuel the fire, light our lamps together, and reaffirm our commission—a commission not simply to come back next week, but to live differently DURING the week. As we continue with Mass this morning, I invite you during the collection to think about the gifts you need to bring to others; during the eucharistic prayer call to mind the names of those who need light and the presence of Christ; during the sign of peace consider who needs your peace and reconciliation; and during communion don't just receive...but in the spirit of Jesus' incredible self-giving, commit yourself to give as well. 'Amen' at communion means not only that 'I believe' but also 'I am committed to live as though I believe.'

"You are salt, light, the fizz in a Coke, the snap in a rubber band, the pop in popcorn," Fr. Zach concluded. "Let your pop, your snap, your fizz resound in the presence of others, that they might know something of the faithful and consoling presence of God." Linda said a silent "Amen"—and wondered if, as a symbol of her new mission to her mother-in-law, she should serve popcorn before dinner tonight!

NOTES

1. "Since at least the early 1970s research data from the National Opinion Research Center have indicated that the Catholic laity rate the caliber of preaching as inferior." Andrew Greeley and Mary Greeley Durkin, *How to Save the Catholic Church* (New York: Viking, 1984), p. 188. "We have asked questions about people's attitudes toward the quality of sermons over the last fifteen years and have found a significant decline in the rating which people assign to the Sunday sermon. The proportion of the population saying that a sermon was excellent has dropped from approximately 44% in the mid-sixties to approximately 20% in the current period." Andrew Greeley, William McCready, and Kathleen McCourt, *Catholic Schools in a Declining Church* (Kansas City: Sheed & Ward, 1976), pp. 110–15; also, William McCready, *Changing Attitudes of American Catholics Toward the Liturgy* (Federation of Diocesan Liturgical Commissions, 1974).

2. Liturgical preaching is employed here as the generic term for preaching in official Roman Catholic worship. While preaching in the eucharist is the most common form of such liturgical preaching, it is not the only form. Preaching during Vespers, for example, or during the celebration of a sacrament outside of eucharist, such as marriage, are also *bona fide* forms of liturgical preaching. In this essay, the term *homily* will be employed as a synonym for liturgical preaching.

3. Burke and Doyle suggest that besides liturgical preaching one can distinguish three other types of preaching: evangelization, which is addressed to those who do not yet believe in Christ (p. 120); catechesis, which focuses on "the living out of the newly professed faith in terms of the customs, tradition, doctrines and practices of the believing community to which the acceptance of the gospel message has brought the believer" (p. 124); and didaskalia, which is a type of preaching that seeks to bring the listener into fullest union with the Trinity (p. 125).

4. *FIYH* was issued without paragraph numberings. Those employed here are according to the numbering that accompanies this document as found in

The Liturgy Documents: A Parish Resource, 3rd ed. (Chicago: Liturgy Training Publications, 1991).

5. The subtitle of the work.

6. Human experience and praxis are not synonymous. The great disparity in usage among various writers makes it difficult to generalize with any accuracy about the differences between the two. In general, however, it might be helpful to think of virtually any experience as "practice," whereas "praxis," in the classic sense given it by Aristotle, is the "action of moral agents guided by some goal of the good and virtuous life and directed to the development of a character possessing phronesis or practical wisdom" (Tracy, 1983, 75). More recently, liberationists like Gustavo Gutierrez have defined praxis as "the lived faith that finds expression in prayer and commitment to social transformation" (1988, xxxiv). A useful overview of theologies of praxis can be found in Tracy (1981, 35–51).

7. As the foreword to *FIYH* notes, Baumer was part of the team that helped to develop this document.

8. *FIYH* provides a seven-step method that such groups could follow in an hour (§108).

9. For a fuller example of such a model of collaborative homily preparation, see my *The Chicago Guide to Preaching* (Chicago: Liturgy Training Publications, forthcoming).

10. Roughly translated as "The prayer of the church is foundational for the belief of the church." The *locus classicus* of this notion is the maxim of Prosper of Aquitaine: *legem credendi lex statuat supplicandi* PL 51:209), for a further discussion of this concept see Paul De Clerck, *"'Lex orandi, lex credendi,' Sens originel et avatars historiques d'un adage équivoque,"* in *Questions liturgiques* 59 (1978): 193–212.

11. In the spirit of *lex orandi, lex orandi,* this could be roughly translated as "the prayer of the church is foundational for the dignity of the church."

REFERENCES

Baumer, Fred A. "Toward the Development of Homiletic as Rhetorical Genre: A Critical Study of Roman Catholic Preaching since Vatican II." Northwestern University: unpublished Ph.D. dissertation, 1985.

Browning, Don. *A Fundamental Practical Theology: Descriptive and Strategic Proposals*. Minneapolis: Fortress Press, 1991.

Burke, John, and Thomas Doyle. *The Homilist's Guide to Scripture, Theology, and Canon Law*. New York: Pueblo Publishing Co., 1986.

Foley, Edward. *Developmental Disabilities and Sacramental Access*. Collegeville, Minn.: The Liturgical Press, 1994.

_____. *Foundations of Christian Music: The Music of Pre-Constantinian Christianity.* Collegeville, Minn.: The Liturgical Press, 1996.

Gutierrez, Gustavo. *A Theology of Liberation*, Revised Edition. Trs. and eds. Caridad Inda and John Eagleson. Maryknoll, N.Y.: Orbis Books, 1988.

Maddox, Randy. "The Recovery of Theology as a Practical Discipline." *Theological Studies* 51 (1990): 650–72.

Postman, Neil. *Amusing Ourselves to Death: Public Discourse in the Age of Show Business.* New York: Viking Penguin, Inc., 1985.

Rahner, Karl. *Theological Investigations* V. Tr. Karl-H. Kruger. Baltimore: Helicon Press, 1966.

_____. *Theological Investigations* XIV. Tr. David Bourke. New York: The Seabury Press, 1976.

Schillebeeckx, Edward. *The Eucharist.* Tr. N.D. Smith. New York: Sheed & Ward, 1968.

Skelley, Michael. *The Liturgy of the World: Karl Rahner's Theology of Worship.* Collegeville, Minn.: The Liturgical Press, 1991.

Sweetser, Thomas, and Patricia Forster. *Transforming the Parish: Models for the Future.* Kansas City: Sheed & Ward, 1993.

Tracy, David, "Theologies of Praxis." *Creativity and Method.* Ed. Matthew L. Lamb. Milwaukee: Marquette University Press, 1981, pp. 35–51.

_____. "The Foundations of Practical Theology." *Practical Theology.* Ed. Don Browning. San Francisco: Harper & Row, 1983, pp. 61–82.

Whitehead, James D., and Evelyn Eaton Whitehead, *Method in Ministry.* Revised Edition. Kansas City: Sheed & Ward, 1995.

ABBREVIATIONS

CSL: Constitution on the Sacred Liturgy
FIYH: Fulfilled in Your Hearing

Immigration Reconsidered in the Context of an Ethic of Solidarity

Patricia A. Lamoureux

America is and has always been a nation of immigrants, shaped and reshaped by successive waves of people drawn to the United States by ideals of democracy and liberty.[1] As a people we proudly boast of the worldwide welcome Lady Liberty offers to those arriving from other lands:

> ...Give me your tired, your poor,
> Your huddled masses yearning to breathe free.
> The wretched refuse of your teeming shore,
> Send these, the homeless, the tempest-tost to me,
> I lift my lamp beside the golden door!

When Emma Lazarus wrote the poem affixed to the copper figure that gazes out over New York Harbor she imagined America as an asylum for the oppressed of all lands. At the time, this vision could be realized because the United States Constitution and the Bill of Rights placed no distinction between citizens and non-citizens except to impose some restrictions on who could hold public office. Without an official policy on immigration, the United States proved to be a magnet for immigrants in the 1800s. Immigration fueled a growing nation, providing farmers for the largely unsettled West and Great Plains as well as factory workers in the growing cities during the Industrial Revolution. Ironically, the installation of the "Mother of Exiles," as Lazarus characterized the Statue of Liberty, roughly coincided with growing doubts about whether an "open door" to all who wanted to enter the U.S. was in the nation's best interest.

A. Fear, Opposition, and Abuse

From the earliest days of the republic, there has been anxiety about the social and political implications of immigration with many Americans ambivalent about the Statue of Liberty's inscription. Thomas Jefferson feared that welcoming the "servile masses of Europe" would transform Americans into a "heterogeneous, incoherent, distracted mass." The earliest wave of Irish, German, and Italian immigrants was viewed as filthy, intemperate, and as a threat that would corrupt the country's heritage. Furthermore, Chinese immigrants were subject to prejudice and especially cruel persecution between 1861 and 1880 when almost 200,000 Chinese came to the United States. Riots in a number of Western towns resulted in the deaths of many Chinese newcomers and state law in California barred them from marrying whites or testifying in court against whites. In short, the nineteenth century began an era of ethnic selectivity with increased and stricter legislation to control legal and illegal immigration. While always somewhat of an anomaly, the "open door" has become a "narrower gate" that has shut out some immigrants entirely. Sanford Ungar, the author of an acclaimed study of new American immigrants notes that "it is ironic, although perhaps not surprising, that the descendants of the earliest immigrants to America have tended to be among the strongest advocates of a restrictive immigration policy" (Unger, 1995, 99).

The reasons for more limited and even exclusionary policies are varied and complex. At the heart of the matter, however, is a dilemma that the influx of new immigrants poses for many Americans. Principles of openness, tolerance, and pluralism are highly valued. Yet, there is a concern that immigration not threaten the livelihood and quality of life of U.S. citizens. U.S. borders seem to be out of control and fears abound that undocumented immigrants are infiltrating the United States to take scarce jobs and access public benefits. The attitude of many, particularly in a state like California that receives inordinately large numbers of immigrants, is summed up incisively by Karol Lindemans, a retired accountant from that state:

> America today is no longer the America of 1954....We had chances and freedom and liberty. Now all that has changed....We're being depleted. Every year we get a huge

bill for our taxes. We don't make TVs, CDs or cars any-
more....We are facing a crisis. We in North America, in
Canada and the U.S., have to brace ourselves for an invasion
from the south....This is not immigration, this is an invasion. (Ungar, 1995, 64)

Such attitudes led to California's Proposition 187, the "Save Our State"
initiative enacted in 1994, which aimed at discouraging and restricting
immigration and the rights of recent immigrants.

In recent years, some of the strongest opposition to immigration
has emerged among the indigenous minority communities in American
cities, especially from African Americans. The resentment is partially
fueled by the threat new immigrants pose to jobs that long-disadvantaged
minorities claim ought to rightfully be theirs. In the words of Moges
Biru, an Ethiopian who has experienced this backlash:

The blacks say to us, "You....foreigners, you came here,
you're making money, you're taking our work." ...They
don't care if we're Ethiopian or African, they just see us as
foreigners. They don't know that I'm a U.S. citizen. What
they see is my face. Or they hear my accent, so they know
that I'm a foreigner. (Unger, 1995, 264)

The black American poet, Wanda Coleman, poignantly summarizes the
tension:

Immigrant populations expect rational behavior from blacks
driven mad by poverty and racism. Blacks expect immigrants to empathize with our plight the minute they set foot
on our turf. Neither side has any chance of getting its way
anytime soon. (Unger, 1995, 365)

For many immigrants, documented and undocumented alike, daily
existence in the "promised land" can be very grim and lonely. They are
often confronted with deplorable living and working conditions as well as
the reality of being aliens in a foreign land without family or other support
system. Immigrants are often exploited by employers who take advantage
of cheap labor. This abuse occurs in the fields where Mexican immigrants, legal or not, are willing to work for a pittance, and in factories

where garment workers endure tedious and long work hours for meager remuneration. Life is less than what Lady Liberty promised and can be very dangerous for those "Mexican-looking" folks driving beat-up cars along the California border. Citizens or not, they are more often stopped, questioned, and sometimes severely mistreated (Unger, 1995, 55, 57). Furthermore, undocumented workers become labeled as criminals and part of the "underclass."

Columbia University sociologist Herbert J. Gans argues that the common metaphor of the underclass implies immoral behavior of those people who have rejected commonly accepted values—illegal immigrants along with street criminals, addicts, hustlers, alcoholics, drifters, the homeless, the mentally ill, welfare recipients, school dropouts, and delinquents. The men of the underclass are assumed to be lazy or ignorant of the importance of work because jobs are available if they wanted to work. Women are imagined to have an unhealthy and immoral taste for sex and for having babies in their teenage years. All are presumed in need of discipline to cure their dependence on welfare or their antisocial activity. Gans argues that what underlies the label of "underclass" is the ideology of "undeservingness" which holds that if people were without the moral and other deficiencies that make them poor, there might be no poverty; if the jobless were not lazy there might be no unemployment. The undeserving are not only the poor, however, but include the outgroup of strangers who, whether actual or imagined, threaten the safety, cultural standards, and economic well-being of better-off Americans (Gans, 1995, 77–90). Such powerful stereotypes blind us to the many ways immigration is an extraordinarily positive feature of American life—that immigrants contribute at least as much as they take. They do work others do not want; they provide models of family life that counter the decline in family structure; and they offer a rich interplay of religion and culture. Furthermore, as Unger's study of immigration reveals, immigrants help the United States maintain its place as an international leader by changing, adapting, and evolving.

I. THE PROBLEM WITH RIGHTS LANGUAGE

Despite Lady Liberty's invitation to the tired, the poor, the homeless, and the wretched refuse, the U.S. remains "a society of strangers," fearful and perplexed over what to do about the "strangers at our gates"

(Ignatieff, 1984, 18, 29). Fears and threats are typically addressed with a particular language. Arguments are made on behalf of more open- or closed-door policies based upon the rights of immigrants, rights of the community, rights of a nation, rights of workers, with the key word being rights. The problem is, however, that rights language, in itself, is insufficient to define, to discuss, or to resolve such a critical issue as immigration. Framing this or any other social controversy in terms of a clash of rights impedes compromise, mutual understanding, and the discovery of common ground. Asserting individual or group rights tends to pit one group against another, group against individual, and group against state. Mary Ann Glendon adroitly sums up the deficiencies of the "American rights dialect" that is characterized by an exaggerated absoluteness, individualism, and is independent of any necessary relation to personal, civic, and collective responsibilities:

> ...we needlessly multiply occasions for civil discord and make it difficult for persons and groups with conflicting interests and views to build coalitions and achieve compromise, or even to acquire the minimal degree of mutual forbearance and understanding that promotes peaceful coexistence and keeps the door open to further communication. Our simplistic rights talk regularly promotes the short-run over the long-term, sporadic crisis intervention over systemic preventive measures, and particular interests over the common good....Lacking a grammar of cooperative living, we are like a traveler who can say a few words to get a meal and a room in a foreign city, but cannot converse with its inhabitants. (Glendon, 1991, 14–15)

Glendon's critique is not an assault on specific rights or on the idea of rights in general. Rather, it is an argument for a richer language and better attitudes than the habitual ways of thinking and speaking about rights. At the core, her argument is about what kind of people we are becoming and what kind of society we are in the process of creating. Indulging in excessively simple forms of rights talk in a pluralistic society "erodes habits, practices and attitudes of respect for others that are the ultimate and surest guarantors of human rights" (Glendon, 1991, 171).

The thesis defended here is that there is a legitimate place for rights language in protecting and promoting human dignity, but a "reconceptualization of rights"[2] is needed. Basically, rights theory "is more helpful in enabling us to denounce violations of human dignity than in guiding us in the design of institutions and pastoral practice which will promote that dignity" (Langan, 1986, 122). The challenge is to uphold the importance of rights as the means for respecting and protecting human dignity while also formulating a "grammar of cooperative living" that rests upon the moral bonds of community.

In the remarks that follow I aim to develop such a grammar drawn from the tradition of Roman Catholic social teaching, that is, the major social encyclicals and episcopal statements of the last one hundred years.[3] Specifically, the language of solidarity, which is the "deep theory"[4] of social teaching, provides the context and framework for the teaching on human rights. By tracing the development of solidarity in the tradition, we can assemble some key elements of an ethic that will facilitate a different way of imagining rights language. In order to note some significant shifts that have occurred in the process of development of this ethic, the documents to be examined will be grouped in three sections: preconciliar, conciliar, and postconciliar. The rights pertaining to migrants and refugees that flow out of this teaching will be emphasized.[5] For "one of the areas in which the church has most persistently advanced the cause of human solidarity is the defense of rights of migrants and refugees" (Christiansen, 1988, 83). As a conclusion, several elements will be proposed that can guide an ethical and pastoral response to the immigration issue.

II. DEVELOPMENT OF AN ETHIC OF SOLIDARITY

A. Foundation of the Ethic

At the core of an ethic of solidarity is the inviolable dignity and sacredness of the human person. Human rights are rooted in this dignity which is "grounded in the concrete universality of each person's ontological solidarity with the human race (Lamb, 1994, 911). While several significant shifts have occurred over the years in the understanding of the human person (Curran, 1986), as well as the theory of human rights (Hollenbach, 1979), two integrally related aspects permeate Catholic social teaching. First, persons *have* dignity, they *are* sacred. Human dignity is not granted or bestowed on persons by family, society, or institutions.

Dignity is a transcendental or ontological characteristic of persons giving them a worth that claims respect in every situation and in every type of activity. It is more fundamental than any specific human right. As an indicative, human dignity makes claims on others that it be recognized and respected. Human rights are the moral imperatives that express the more specific context of these claims. Because the process of identifying the concrete claims of human dignity is continually changing, the task of identifying the rights or conditions for the realization of human worth is also an ongoing process (Hollenbach, 1979, 90–92). Second, human persons are social, relational beings. Because of the essentially social nature of human dignity, the uniqueness and dignity of the person always exists in the context of relations in a larger community. Life in community is the context in which human dignity and rights are protected and expanded. As Philip Land remarked in his reflections on over a half a century of work on official church teaching, "Rights are possessed, shared, promoted, guaranteed in and through the existence of commonality, communal being, and solidarity" (Land, 1994, 72).

While human rights clearly is a consistent and significant theme in Catholic social teaching, Michael Schuck persuasively argues it is not the "theory of coherence" that integrates the many principles and values inherent in the tradition. Rather, papal teaching coheres around a theologically inspired communitarian social ethic: "Internal to all the popes' social recommendations and judgments is a communitarian understanding of the self and society....In the papal view, mutuality is a characteristic of embedded selves. This quality, in turn, defines society" (Schuck, 1994, 187). Michael and Kenneth Himes similarly argue that the appropriate understanding of human rights in Catholic social teaching is within a communitarian vision. They write: "The most fundamental human right is the right to exercise the power of self-giving, the opportunity for entrance into relationship, for deeper participation in the life of the human community" (Himes and Himes, 1993, 61). In this framework, there is an acknowledgment of true mutuality which is diminished by the denial of rights or the exclusion of some people in the life of the communities. In Catholic social teaching a just society is one in which humans exist in right relationship to one another and this entails more than the regulation of personal rights. It requires the experience of communities that practice forgiveness, mutual respect, honor, and love. Thus, "while rights must be met in any true community, there is more that is necessary.

For we are more than bearers of rights. Our rights may be respected and yet our true dignity denied. Belonging, respect, friendship, forgiveness, love are essential to human well-being, but they are not easily addressed by the language of rights" (Himes, 1993, 169). A communitarian vision inspires a language of solidarity which begins to take shape in the preconciliar writings of Popes Leo XIII, Pius XI, and Pius XII.

B. Preconciliar Teachings: Organic Solidarity

In the preconciliar writings of Popes Leo XIII, Pius XI, and Pius XII we find an "organic solidarity" (Hollenbach, 1979, 161) based on the philosophy of solidarism, an organic conception of society that emphasizes how various members are part of and related to the whole along the lines of how the parts of the human body interact. This outlook is drawn from the medieval sense of unity and strong sense of community. Solidarism is a hierarchical model of social interaction that highlights the structural harmonies and organic unities of social life while minimizing institutional strains and social conflict. It is a "third way," removed from extremes of nineteenth-century liberal capitalism that exalted individual choice and interest over common bonds with responsibility for others, and a kind of socialism which subordinated individual liberty to social well-being without respect for human rights or religious welfare. In contrast, the popes emphasized cooperation and harmony. They spoke a resounding no to an excessive individualism and the espousal of rights of liberty without corresponding duties that broke up a larger solidarity (Coleman and Baum, 1991, vii).

1. Rights in a Harmonious Community

Leo XIII imagined classes living in a mutually interdependent order and harmony, motivated by charity and justice with a realization of the primacy of duties each class had toward the other, rather than the rights each class claimed over and against the other. As David Hollenbach maintains, Leo "viewed the boundaries of such a society like a solid mold into which the precious but fluid element of dignity is poured in order to give it structure and shape....Thus both the interrelations between rights and the means for institutionalizing rights are influenced by this taken-for-granted social order" (Hollenbach, 1979, 92–93). The issue of migration is to be considered within this structural harmony, for Leo believed that when people have a chance to acquire property and work the land that is theirs "they cling to the country in which they were born; for no one would exchange his country for a foreign land if his own afforded him the means of living a tolerable and happy life" (RN 35).[6] In other words, there is a relationship between the decision to emigrate, social harmony, and participation in the economic life of a nation.

In response to the "wretchedness and misery" to which workers were being subjected, Leo XIII advocated worker and employer participation in trade associations and other intermediate associations, especially those with religious affiliations (RN 36–42). He argued that rich and poor should be united in bonds of friendship and love because of their common dignity as children of God. The poor, however, have a claim to special consideration and the state has a special obligation to defend the rights of the poor and powerless. The role of the church is to intervene directly on behalf of the poor when it perceives efficacious action in the relief of poverty (RN 21, 24, 36). For Leo, "the aim was to eliminate poverty altogether, not merely by the temporary expedient of charity but by a permanent readjustment in workers' standard of living and position in society" (Camp, 1986, 34).

2. Mutual Cooperation and Responsibilities

For Pius XI, organic solidarity requires mutually cooperative responsibilities of owners, managers, workers, and the state for the promotion of the common good. In calling for these intermediate associations both Leo and Pius are appealing to the principle of subsidiarity, which can be found, in some form, in nearly every major social document of the tradition. Given its classic formulation by Pius XI in *Quadragesimo Anno,* his encyclical commemorating the fortieth anniversary of *Rerum Novarum,* subsidiarity means that "it is a serious evil and a perturbation of right order to assign to a larger and higher society what can be performed successfully by smaller and lower communities (QA 79). Government intervention is justified when it truly provides help to those smaller communities that compose society or whenever it is necessary for the remedy of harm or the promotion of the common good.

Pius XI was reacting to the pervasive violations of human dignity that were the result of the great depression and the economic structures that lay behind this situation of worldwide poverty. While Leo merely hinted at the requirement of social justice, it is prominent in the writings of Pius XI. There is a shift in focus to institutional structures of society that must be developed in such a way that basic rights are protected. This shift was an important development since it began a process by which the institutional order was perceived as flexible and subject to change (Hollenbach, 1979, 93). The standard of social justice that Pius XI emphasized was the basis of his call for the enactment of social legislation to enable cooperation among all people engaged in industry or professions for their mutual benefit and for the good of the whole economy.

3. Spirit of Fraternity

Like his predecessors, Pius XII envisaged an organically united society but the extrinsic, static relations between personal dignity and the social structures that protect it almost entirely vanished. As he identified it on a number of occasions, society was to be a "community of morally responsible citizens" with a respect for the common good grounded in obligations of solidarity. This form of human interrelationship was necessary, in Pius's mind, in order to address the problem of "depersonalization," the treatment of people as "mere material objects" with little regard for their dignity and rights. Solidarity, "a sincere spirit of fraternity uniting all classes," is the moral principle upon which society is to be built (Yzermans, vol II, 1961, 20). Solidarity demands "that outrageous and provoking inequalities in living standards among different groups in a nation be eliminated;…that everything possible be done to maintain and increase employment within nations;…and that among nations there is 'international solidarity' which demands the abolition of inequalities in living standards" (Yzermans, vol. II, 1961, 165–66).

From a community of mutually responsible citizens with obligations of solidarity emerge the rights of people to emigrate. Pius argued that there is a "natural right of the individual to be unhampered in immigration or emigration which is not recognized or, in practice, is nullified under the pretext of a common good which is falsely understood or applied, but sanctioned and made mandatory by legislative or administrative measures" (Yzermans, vol II, 1961, 167). Furthermore, the pope spoke of "the right of a family to a vital space" or to land that is agriculturally productive in order to satisfy proper needs. Migration permits the exercise of this important family right and thus benefits both the country of emigration, which may be overcrowded and lacking in available property as well as the country of immigration, which profits by gaining stable and industrious citizens (Yzermans, 1961, 34). The hope for realization of a such a community, however, requires more than the enforcement of human rights. That is, there needs to be the inculcation of trust and love in accord with justice, equity, and prudence in order to realize the obligations of solidarity In Pius's mind this is not merely an idealistic vision but a realizable moral imperative.

In sum, the preconciliar writings reveal an understanding of solidarity that is organic and conflict-free. It presumes a mutually interdependent order of cooperation and harmony of interests between all groups and classes in society, motivated by charity and justice. The poor, however, have special claims when there exist inordinate amounts of inequality. Where Leo XIII's focus is on worker solidarity and duties based on class in a hierarchically ordered society, Pius XI envisions mutually cooperative responsibilities among groups in society. Not only justice among groups in society is needed, but also social justice, which requires institutional structures to protect basic rights in accord with the common good. Pius XII began to push the vision into the wider arena of international solidarity with obligations that require not only improvement of material conditions but the formation of mutually responsible citizens. In this earliest stage of the ethic, economic rights, in particular, are recognized as essential to protect human dignity. Virtues of love, trust, justice, prudence along with principles of equity, subsidiarity, and participation are needed as well to promote a vision of organic solidarity. Moreover, the rich and poor are to be united in bonds of friendships because of their common dignity.

C. Conciliar Teachings: Global Solidarity

With the conciliar-era documents of John XXIII and Vatican II there is a breakdown of organic solidarity due to the growing awareness of historicity and the contextual, dynamic, conflictual nature of social problems. Furthermore, advances in social organization and technological developments as well as the increasing interdependence of people and nations led to a more global vision of solidarity. With global solidarity society is envisioned as a community of persons who participate in and cooperate with others at the local, national, and international levels in order to attain the common good. While not a new theme in the tradition, the common good is most clearly linked with human dignity and global solidarity by John XXIII. As John defines it, the common good is the sum total of those conditions of social living, whereby people are enabled more fully and more readily to achieve their own perfection. The common good is not just a summation of the goods of individual citizens but incorporates the demands of justice in organizing and structuring economic life so that human dignity is preserved and promoted (MM 65, 83). While maintaining the traditional view that society exists for the benefit of the human person, John adds a "significantly new emphasis" by moving toward a definition of human dignity in social and structural terms. "Consequently, the call of human dignity as a moral demand now addresses human beings in association in a significantly more important way than was pointed out by previous papal documents" (Hollenbach, 1979, 63).

The common good may also require some to relinquish their privileges for the sake of the social good in which they share and which secures their own rights. This may be necessary in order to ensure the rights of "the less fortunate members of the community since they are less able to defend their rights and to assert their legitimate claims" (PT 56). This is so because exclusion or marginalization of some people in society injures the common good. In essence, rights can not exist apart from the common good "because individual rights exist in solidarity. The good of the commonality is the sine qua non for the actualization of individual rights" (Land, 1994, 71). Moreover, the individual and the common good ought not to be pitted against each other because the need for some people to sacrifice for others is to enrich them as mature members of society.

1. Connectedness and Contextualization of Rights

In the most comprehensive treatment of rights that is found in Catholic social teaching, John XXIII brings together the rights defended in previous documents of the tradition and enlarges the domain of rights according to the vision of global solidarity. In *Pacem in Terris* the pope enumerates the human rights necessary for the good order of society based upon an anthropology that stresses both the unity of the human person as a being in the world and as one who is oriented to society and community. This systematic recapitulation of rights claims include rights to life and an adequate standard of living such as the rights to bodily integrity, food, clothing, shelter, rest, medical care, necessary social services, security in cases of sickness, old age, or unemployment; rights in the area of religious activity and family life; economic rights including the right to work, to humane working conditions, to a just wage; the right to private property with appropriate social obligations; the right of assembly and association; political rights of participation in public affairs (PT 11–27). These are "rights of persons in community" that exist as claims of human dignity in relations between persons, society, and nations. Corresponding to rights are duties and responsibilities that are the result of the interdependence of persons upon one another. Thus, "it is clear that a right or any given set of single rights is not to be conceived of as the atomic building blocks of the moral universe" (Hollenbach, 1979, 65–66, 179).

Global solidarity requires that refugees and migrants have the right to enter a political community where the possibility exists of more fittingly providing for a better future for oneself and one's family. John insists that "every human being has the right to emigrate to other countries and take up residence there when there are just reasons for it" (PT 25). It is the duty of the state to accept immigrants and help their integration as new members of society. Further, refugees cannot lose these rights simply because they are deprived of citizenship of their own states (PT 105, 106). The rights to emigrate and immigrate exist because "the fact that one is a citizen of a particular state does not detract in any way from membership in the human family as a whole, nor from citizenship in the world community" (PT 23). Thus, the right to emigrate is founded on the basis of one's humanity, not citizenship, and the immigrant retains that right which must be respected by all people and societies.

Solidarity and the promotion of the common good, however, does not exclude regulation of emigration and immigration at national and international levels. "Operative in John's thinking was a human right to asylum for legitimate refugees which ought to be respected and a conditional right to naturalization for those refugees in a host country. The latter right is contextualized by the common good of the host society. But the former right, that of asylum, seems to be a stronger claim with no stated condition" (Himes, 1996, 29). The control of emigration, though, "even when it is for the common good of a particular country, cannot ignore the universal destination of earthly goods and the gospel demand for solidarity among peoples" (Blume, 1996, 8). The bottom line: solidarity requires that adequate solutions to migration and refugee questions be reached through international cooperation and mutual understanding (MM 45).

2. Unity of the Human Family

The Second Vatican Council's document *Gaudium et Spes* embraces the vision of global solidarity which flows from a common brotherhood/sisterhood in Christ. This is a "solidarity with the entire human family" which is a "needful solidarity" because of the growing interdependence of people and society as well as the many conflicting forces that separate and divide rather than encourage cooperation and dialogue (GS 3,4,23–25, 32). Here, the bishops give solidarity a more theological emphasis and stress the unity of the human family. They write of unity as that which belongs to the innermost nature of the church, as a "sacramental sign," and an instrument of intimate union with God and with all humankind (GS 42). The church reflects Christ to the world "most of all by her healing and elevating impact on the dignity of the human person, by the way in which she strengthens the seams of human society" (GS 40). Thus, the defense of the dignity of the person and building up the unity of the human family converge in "promoting the rights of all persons, irrespective of nationality" (GS 42).

Gaudium et Spes provides the fullest and most comprehensive understanding of the dignity of the human person which serves as the "cornerstone" of the document (Curran, 1986, 196). The objective criterion for determining the moral character of activity is the dignity of the human person "integrally and adequately considered"[7] (Janssens, 1980–81, 13). By this phrase is meant that an appropriate anthropology considers the human person as a historical subject in corporeality who stands in relation to other persons, to social structures, to the world, and to God; who is a unique originality yet fundamentally equal with all other persons; and who has a transcendental dignity to be reverenced (GS 12–32, 76). The dignity of the human person generates universal and inviolable rights and duties which have been articulated most fully by John XXIII. The council adds nothing to these but stresses social, economic, and cultural rights along with responsibility, participation, dialogue, and organized action to promote these rights (GS 70–74).

Regarding the question of immigration considered in the context of global solidarity, more than rights need to be considered. Essentially, immigrants must be treated "not as mere tools of production but as persons." They ought to be helped in their efforts to bring their families to live with them and to provide themselves with a decent dwelling. Immigrants should be protected from discrimination, long working hours, inadequate living conditions, and exclusion or marginalization from social and political life. Justice and equity require that "when workers come from another country or district and contribute by their labor to the economic advancement of a nation or region, all discrimination with respect to wages and working conditions must be carefully avoided" (GS 66). Workers must also be incorporated into the social life of the country or region that received them. Employment opportunities, however, should be created in their own native areas as far as possible.

In sum, with the conciliar documents there is a growing awareness of the interdependence of people and nations as well as a historical, dynamic view of society. This leads to a shift from organic solidarity to a more global vision. John XXIII develops the notion of the common good and emphasizes just international structures to enable persons to exercise their rights, to fulfill their duties, and to become actively involved in the process of promoting solidarity. The scope of rights is expanded to include political, social, and cultural rights as well as individual and economic rights. Based upon the unity of the human family, the dignity and rights of all persons adequately and integrally considered must be protected and promoted. The meaning of solidarity now encompasses mutual bonding, cooperation, and participation with others at the local, national, and international levels to attain the common good.

D. Postconciliar Teachings: Spirit of Solidarity

The postconciliar writings of Paul VI and *Justice in the World*, the document that emerged from the synod that Paul convened, reflect a response to a "crisis" of global solidarity. This refers to the worldwide connectedness of social problems and the growing inequality between and within nations that breaks down bonds of solidarity. Paul VI argues for "integral development" to be achieved in a "spirit of solidarity," which means mutual understanding and friendship flowing from the sacred communion of all people made in the image and likeness of God. To be considered "authentic" or "integral," development has to promote the good of all people and foster personal and communal development. There should be opportunities for participation in processes of decision making and involvement of the people themselves in development through their own work. Integral development requires movement from less human conditions, that is, lack of material necessities and oppressive social structures to conditions that are more human, that is, possession of necessities, growth of knowledge, acquisition of culture, increased esteem for the dignity of others, cooperation for the common good, the will and desire for peace, the acknowledgment of supreme values of love and friendship, prayer and contemplation (PP 14–21, 76–80). In addition, the work of development is to draw nations together in dialogue in the attainment of goals pursued with a common effort, inspired by love, and motivated by the sincere desire to build a "civilization founded on world solidarity" (PP 66–73).

1. Duties of Solidarity

The spirit of solidarity implies the duty of rich nations to give aid to developing countries, the duty of social justice, and the duty of universal charity (PP 43–44). Aid for the weaker members of the human family, those ravaged by hunger and poverty, requires more than private and public funds given to remove people from destitution. Rather, the aim is to create a world where every person can live a more fully human life, freed from various forms of servitude and oppression.

The duty of social justice has to do with equity in trade relations, with economic and political structures that are more just and better organized toward a universal solidarity. Such a vision prohibits excessive nationalism, which isolates people, and racism, which not only denigrates human dignity but is an obstacle to collaboration among disadvantaged nations and a cause of division and hatred within countries (PP 56–63).

The duty of universal charity requires hospitality, the creation of centers of welcome to protect people, especially migrant workers, who often live in inhuman conditions and who suffer from loneliness or feelings of abandonment (PP 69). Migrants deserve special attention because, in spite of their participation in the economy of the country that receives them, they are often marginalized or excluded from the social life and benefits of the community. Solidarity requires individuals and groups to go beyond a narrowly nationalist attitude and to assure people a right to emigrate, favor their integration, facilitate their professional advancement, and give them access to decent housing (OA 17).

In short, it is the duty of all, but especially that of Christians, to work for solidarity that requires the privileged and powerful to use their resources to benefit the lives of the unfortunate and oppressed. Drew Christiansen maintains that from the point of view of normative ethics, Paul VI's specification of "duties of solidarity" was the most important step in the use of the language of solidarity (Christiansen, 1984, 663).

Implied in these "duties" is a call to action. Thus, Paul VI insists that "it is not enough to recall principles, state intentions, point to crying injustices, and utter prophetic denunciations." These words will lack real weight unless they are accompanied by a better awareness of personal responsibility, collaboration, and effective action. Paul believes that as people accept and live out these duties they will gradually begin to experience true freedom which is not simply a claim for autonomy, but a freedom to be in relationship with God and neighbor, creating bonds of solidarity (OA, 47–48).

2. *Solidaristic Equality*

In response to the "crisis of universal solidarity" the bishops in *Justice in the World* focus on the necessity of just social structures and relationships among people, especially with the poor and the oppressed. They note that injustice is particularly evident in regard to the treatment of migrants who are often forced to leave their own country to find work, but frequently confront "closed doors," discriminatory attitudes, or inhumane treatment when they are allowed to enter another country (JW 289, 292). As a response to the crisis of solidarity marked by injustice the bishops stress the right to development.

The right to development is defined as "a dynamic interpenetration of all those fundamental human rights upon which the aspirations of individuals and nations are based (JW 290). As David Hollenbach points out, this right is not to be regarded simply as an additional right to be added to those accumulated from previous documents. Rather, the right to development clarifies the tradition's understanding of how the content of rights is to be determined: "The right to development affirms that both personal activity and institutional organization are to be directed to the creation of a social order in which persons are able to realize their personal rights in mutuality and solidarity with each other" (Hollenbach, 1979, 85, 100). In addition, the right to development is a "comparative right." That is to say, its concrete content can only be discovered by considering the individual person within his or her social context in relation to other persons. The comparative nature of the right refers to the standard of participation which can be used to determine when human dignity is being supported or violated by complex social structures. Participation is the condition for the realization of human potentialities, none of which can or will be realized as long as persons remain in a condition of extreme marginalization and powerlessness (Hollenbach, 1979, 87–89). In short, at the center of these teachings is "solidaristic equality" which gives a unity and focus to the rights and duties as well as the notion of integral development (Christiansen, 1984, 653).

The most comprehensive treatment of solidarity is found in the writings of John Paul II. In his encyclical *Evangelium Vitae,* the pope challenges all people, especially the Catholic community, to collectively build and maintain an ethic of solidarity (EV 5). To understand what John Paul means by an ethic of solidarity, it is necessary to examine several of his social encyclicals. For the theme of solidarity permeates his writings and each document provides some elements that need to be considered collectively in order to grasp the complexity and comprehensiveness of the ethic he advocates.

At the heart of what he perceives to be a "culture of death," is an attitudinal problem, a lack of solidarity. Human life is easily denigrated; the weakest members of society are viewed as disposable; and the rights and duties that are inherent in his or her dignity are too readily denied. A "breach of solidarity" leads to the need to control life and death along with a disregard for those who are useless in society. Also indicative of a lack of solidarity is the growing gap between wealthy and poor individuals and nations that has grown dramatically over the last decade (CA 26). In essence, the relationship between humankind and God is deformed by attitudes of distrust and hostility rather than communion (EV 36).

It is the lack of solidarity that often provokes emigration, for when people are denied economic initiative, when the creative subjectivity of the citizen is destroyed by an overly bureaucratic state, "this provokes a sense of frustration or desperation and predisposes people to opt out of national life, impelling many to emigrate and also favoring a form of 'psychological' emigration" (SRS 15).

3. Cultivation of Virtue

For John Paul, solidarity is a moral attitude or virtue,[8] which is defined as "a firm and persevering determination to commit oneself to the common good...because we are all responsible for all" (SRS 38). As a Christian virtue, solidarity is integrally related to charity; it "seeks to go beyond itself, to take on the specifically Christian dimension of total gratuity, forgiveness and reconciliation....It is clearly linked to the Christian ideal of unity or communion. This unity reflects the intimate life of the Trinity and discloses a new model of the human race, which must ultimately inspire our solidarity" (SRS 40). The virtue of solidarity unites love and justice and binds us to those who are close to us, to society as a whole, and to the world community. In addition, without mercy justice tends to become formal and legalistic. Mercy is necessary to lead justice beyond an external restoration of rights to the experience of reconciliation and solidarity. The pope writes: "It is impossible to establish a bond between people if they wish to regulate their mutual relationships solely according to the measure of justice" (DM 14). Mercy does not consist only in compassion but is most fully manifested when it restores the experience of value to one who has come to feel a loss of dignity. "Appreciation of the dignity of the person is what keeps expressions of mercy from degrading the person, primarily by establishing the communality of a relationship" (Dorr, 1992, 349). Thus, mercy and love complement justice, enabling people to meet and value one another appreciative of one another's human dignity.

While solidarity includes justice, mercy, and universal love, it also requires an "option or love of preference for the poor," a special form of primacy in exercise of Christian charity. The option for the poor embraces the immense multitudes of the hungry, needy, homeless, those without medical care and above all, those without hope of a better future. From this absolute imperative emerge specific norms for individual action and social responsibilities. The growing numbers of poor in desperate situations must be a priority in all development plans. Solidarity necessitates, on the part of the powerful, a responsibility and willingness to share; on the part of the weaker, an active claiming of rights based upon their human dignity (SRS 42). Furthermore, the more individuals and groups are defenseless within a given society, the more they require the care and concern of others, and in particular the intervention of governmental authority to ensure that basic human rights are protected (CA 46).

4. Civilization of Love

In even stronger language than previous popes, John Paul links authentic development, solidarity, and respect for human rights. As Donal Dorr writes: "John Paul's teaching on solidarity is designed to plug a notable gap that often arises when personal development is put at the heart of a system of morality. This gap is the one between the individual's claim for rights and the others with whom that person is linked in any way" (Dorr, 1989, 146–147). Authentic human development must be achieved within the framework of solidarity and freedom, based on love of God and neighbor, and must help to promote the relationship between individuals and society or what can be called a "civilization of love." This has four implications. First, it implies an awareness of the value of the rights of all and of each person as well as the need to respect these rights. Second, respect for all rights takes on great importance, especially the right to life at every stage of existence; the rights of the family; the rights inherent in the life of the political community; the rights based on the transcendent vocation of the human person, such as the right to freedom to profess and practice one's religious belief. Third, on the international level there must be respect for the identity and fundamental equality of people, with their unique historical and cultural characteristics. Fourth, there must be respect for the cosmos and an awareness of the mutual connection of beings, whether living or inanimate, recognizing the limitations of natural resources. In short, authentic development is measured by the degree to which solidarity and the respect for human rights—personal, social, economic, political, and ecological—are evident (SRS 32,33). Solidarity helps us to see the "other"—whether a person, people, nation, or the cosmos—not just as some kind of instrument to be exploited and discarded when no longer useful, but a partner in the banquet of life to which all are equally invited by God (SRS 39).

John Paul calls attention to the rights of migrants who are often subject to exploitation and degradation. He insists that people have the right to leave their native land for various motives, as well as the right to return, in order to seek better living conditions in another country. In stating this, he recognizes emigration as a "necessary evil" riddled with difficulties. It is a loss for the country left behind as well as for the persons who, for one reason or another, must leave their homeland and begin life anew often in the midst of an alien society with its foreign culture and language. Further, this pope advocates just legislation with regard to the rights of migrant workers to ensure that they are not exploited or placed at a disadvantage in comparison with other workers in that society. He writes: "The value of work should be measured by the same standard and not according to the difference in nationality, religion, or race...and the profound meaning of work itself requires that capital should be at the service of labor and not labor at the service of capital" (LE 23).

5. *Union, Dialogue, and Collaboration*

In accord with Pope Leo's landmark encyclical, *Rerum Novarum,* and in commemoration of its one hundredth anniversary, John Paul II calls for "worker solidarity" together with a clearer and more committed realization by others of workers' rights understood in the broader context of human rights. Work is both an obligation and a source of rights, including the right to just wages and other social benefits (LE 16,17). The pope notes that despite many positive advances in the conditions of labor since the writings of Leo XIII, there remain violations of the dignity of human work. In some cases, injustices have grown worse because workers' solidarity is not grounded in work's authentic, human meaning. Thus, "in order to achieve social justice in various parts of the world...there is a need for ever new movements of solidarity of the workers and with the workers. This solidarity must be present whenever it is called for by the social degrading of the subject of work, by exploitation of the workers and by the growing areas of poverty and even hunger" (LE 8). Labor unions are necessary to express solidarity in defending workers' rights and can be the vehicle for active participation in humanizing work. If properly oriented toward the common good, unions present an opportunity for a "wider solidarity of *all* who work....It is clear that even if it is because of their work needs that people unite to secure their rights, their union remains a constructive factor of social order and solidarity" (LE 20).

This understanding of solidarity is not a "solidarity-against" but a constructive "solidarity-for" and requires dialogue and collaboration (Sorge, 1986, 244–46). For John Paul, collaboration is important in achieving solidarity because it is a process in which conflict, opposition, and some efforts toward consensus in decision making have to be achieved. Forming relationships of mutual trust, respect, and reciprocity through dialogue is one of the most important aspects of collaboration. Only with continued dialogue can there be an opportunity to work together and find solutions. Without dialogue the collaborative effort ceases, eliminating the possibility for solidarity and resulting in separation, division, or alienation. Collaboration and good dialogue require the ability to listen to the other in mutual respect. As an element of solidarity, collaboration requires listening, especially to the voices of poor people and nations. Furthermore, the poorest nations or individuals, as well, are not exempt from this task but must do what they can with their talents and gifts to serve the wider community (Bilgrien, 1995, 98–103).

In sum, the postconciliar teachings shift the emphasis further in the direction of spirituality and virtue. This evolution reveals most clearly the inadequacy of rights language in itself to address social problems and threats to human dignity. Paul VI links integral development with a "spirit of solidarity" which implies duties of rich nations to aid developing countries, the duty of social justice, and the duty of universal charity. The ethic of solidarity that John Paul II advances requires an attitudinal change from a lack of respect and responsibility for human life, society, and the ecology to a firm, persevering determination to commit oneself to the common good. Solidarity is integrally related to the virtues of charity, mercy, and justice, and as a Christian virtue, it is linked to the Christian ideal of communion. The ethic implies the formation of relationships of mutual trust, respect, and understanding to be achieved through collaboration and dialogue. There is a strong emphasis of the priority of the poor and those who are most defenseless in society to receive more care and government protection.

III. POLICY AND PASTORAL IMPLICATIONS

From this ethic of solidarity several policy and pastoral implications regarding the issue of migration can be formulated.

1. A commitment to solidarity according to Catholic social teaching raises questions for two important areas of present immigration policy. First, solidarity requires avoiding discrimination against the poor. The present policy gives priority to women and men with certain skills or qualifications that make them attractive in a highly technological and competitive free-market economy. That immediate economic advantage should play such a significant part in determining who is or is not admitted to this nation seems to fail a concern for genuine solidarity with the disadvantaged. A second question for the present policy is the exclusion of economic distress from the definition of those who qualify as refugees. Present policy gives priority to those whose civil and political liberties are in grave and immediate risk. Without denying the correctness of granting political refugees admission to the U.S., solidarity would expand what conditions ought to count for refugee status to include grave and serious threats to socioeconomic rights.

2. The reality of poverty requires efforts to help prevent economic migration, where possible, through international cooperation and policies that are based on integral or authentic development. Solidarity requires a broader understanding of the root causes of migrations, a clearer acceptance of international responsibility, and a willingness to address the causes that lead people to leave their homeland. In their *Pastoral Statement on Migrants and Refugees* the bishops stress the importance of understanding the root causes of migrations:

> In the interrelated and interdependent community of nations, our policy decisions concerning foreign relations, trade, and economic and social development bear directly on the movements of peoples. These decisions should be directed in such a way as to facilltate the right of people to remain in their homelands where they may find a decent standard of living and where their basic needs are met. The advocacy, however, of the right to stay in one's country should not be used as an excuse to deny the right to migrate....Current legislation

must, therefore, reflect our best traditions which the Statue of Liberty continues to symbolize: the ongoing American democratic experiment, our past achievements and our current welcome to newcomers. (NCCB, 1986, 11)

3. There is a legitimate role for government intervention to support claims of immigrants who are presently denied access to public goods, and who are excluded from economic or political participation in the community. The principle of subsidiarity supports the primacy of intermediary associations such as labor unions, community organization, and other forms of support and advocacy at the state or local levels. This does not mean, however, that the federal government ought to ignore its legitimate responsibility to protect the well-being of all residents and promote the public good. When the smaller communities need help or if the common good is being harmed, government intervention is justified.

4. The right to immigrate may be limited in view of the common good, when such goods as communal integrity, cultural ideals, and material well-being are threatened by too many immigrants. The human right to emigrate is not to be equated with the right to immigrate, which is valid but can be regulated. For example, a nation may have to regulate immigration in order to meet its obligations to those already within its borders (Himes, 1996, 29). Furthermore, some states, like California which is impacted by immigration to a greater degree than other areas, may require special assistance from the federal government. In any case, the exclusion of immigration ought not be a matter of general practice.

5. An ethic of solidarity that includes justice, charity, and mercy does not allow turning our borders into militarized zones and denying basic human services to people once within our borders. Such punitive actions would be unjust, for immigrants have rights, even those who are undocumented, to basic goods, such as education, health care, and housing. Undocumented immigrants and their families are legally "non-persons," vulnerable to exploitation, prejudice, and raids at places of work resulting in fear and intimidation. In the spirit of solidarity fair and reasonable processes should be created whereby basic services are provided for all residing within the borders of the United States.

6. The solidaristic equality aimed at in Catholic social teaching is not an absolute or leveling kind of equality implying that everyone in society receive the same benefits and share the same burdens. For example, citizens of a nation do have different rights than legal immigrants who are not citizens and undocumented immigrants. Rather, what is called for is "relative equality." This means that "inequalities are held within a defined range set by moral limits" such as need, hardship, the common good. Limits are set on the permissible differences in order to maintain bonds of solidarity and ensure that men and women treat one another as brothers and sisters (Christiansen, 1984, 653–54).

7. While an ethic of solidarity incorporates some principles and norms of judgment, communities of discernment are required to analyze the situation that is proper to each country, to shed on it the light of the gospel, and to provide directives for action (OA 4). Central to the process of discernment is reflection on experience. Regarding questions of immigration, the experiences and stories of immigrants ought to be included. For too often policy or pastoral decisions are made by people who have no contact with immigrants and lack knowledge of what happens to them after they arrive. Most frequently neglected are the experiences of women immigrants who often assume responsibility for the care of family as well as participating in the work force while trying to adjust to the difficulties of being in a strange land. Moreover, it is from the experiences of solidarity that bonds of affection, friendship, and commitment can develop.

8. At the heart of the ethic is the need for change of attitude, viewing the stranger as gift rather than threat. The newcomer brings cultural values and an ethos that can enhance our American way of life. For example, many ethnic groups have maintained a strong sense of family and community that can help to counter the individualism that characterizes U.S. society and that is, at least in part, responsible for the crisis of solidarity we presently confront. Importantly, as James Dalton's article points out, it is within a context of crosscultural dialogue, in solidarity with our brothers and sisters of different faiths, that ideas of human dignity and human rights can be enriched and best understood. While attitudinal change does not occur easily, negative stereotypes and images can be transformed through dialogue and mutually enriching encounters.

Another way to foster the attitude of solidarity is through worship, the regular engagement in stories and ritual that shapes how we are disposed toward and view the world. For, "when the Church gathers it does so in order to imagine what the world would be like if we believed that the justice of God has become flesh; to rehearse the justice of God until we get it right" (Koernke, 1992, 37). And, in explaining the difference in preaching *about* dignity and preaching *with* dignity, Edward Foley demonstrates how liturgical preaching can foster the attitude of solidarity. Not only does liturgical preaching rehearse what it believes about the dignity of the baptized but it brings us into solidarity with all humanity and, by implication, rehearses the dignity of the human family enmeshed in the liturgy of the world.

9. Centers of welcome for immigrants should be established to respond to feelings of loneliness and isolation that accompany immigrants. With an attitude of solidarity "xenophobia" is replaced with "philoxenia," which means friendship for strangers, or hospitality (Blume, 1996, 10, 11, 19). The hospitality called for includes helping to free immigrants from situations of isolation, to try to reunite them with families, and to help them regain hope and confidence. Those already participating in vibrant and sound communal relations need to reach out to those who are marginalized or excluded in order to create a truly participatory community.

CONCLUSION

From the corpus of Catholic social teaching examined we can conclude that an ethic of solidarity is first and foremost an ethic of character. It has to do with the kind of people we are and hope to become—people formed with dispositions of charity, mercy, and justice united in bonds of mutual trust and friendship. Solidarity is a way of viewing the world as a mutually interdependent global community of responsible citizens. In this ethic, being and doing are integrally connected. We become people of solidarity through participation in public life, through acts of cooperation and collaboration, by promoting the common good, by defending and promoting the dignity and rights of all people, especially the more defenseless in society who take precedence in care and concern. Furthermore, an ethic of solidarity provides a grammar for cooperative living that rests upon the moral bonds of community. As such, it reconceptualizes rights language in a way that is more inclusive and relational than when viewed through the lens of autonomy. It is a grammar that embraces the language of Lady Liberty but adds new dimensions. The tired, the poor, and the tempest-tossed to whom we offer welcome are also bearers of new cultural expressions in the American mosaic. The new immigrants for whom we "lift the lamp beside the golden door" and offer welcome are not only the huddled masses and the homeless, but also those with whom we share a common dignity and bond.

NOTES

1. I will use United States and America interchangeably to avoid constant repetition throughout the paper. In doing so, I recognize that Canadians and Mexicans are also people of the North American continent. I mean no disparagement of these two nations when I use the term America as synonymous with U.S.

2. The phrase "reconceptualization of rights" is borrowed from Arthur J. Dyck, *Rethinking Rights and Responsibilities: The Moral Bonds of Community* (Ohio: Pilgrim Press, 1994). Dyck argues, as I do, that rights need to be grounded in the moral requisites of community and in moral responsibilities, that is, relations or bonds between individuals and groups. Excessive focus on rights tends to obscure or even undermine the human bonds that naturally give rise to and sustain families and communities which are the means to actualize human rights.

3. While there is a corpus of papal encyclicals dating from 1740, *On the Condition of Labor*, written in 1891 by Pope Leo XIII, represents a kind of "magna carta" for modern Catholic social thought.

With the exceptions of the Vatican II document, *Pastoral Constitution on the Church in the Modern World,* and *Justice in the World,* the document produced by the synod of bishops convened by Pope Paul VI, the focus in this essay will be on the social encyclicals. All citations from papal and conciliar documents, unless otherwise indicated, are taken from David J. O'Brien and Thomas A. Shannon, eds., *Catholic Social Thought: The Documentary Heritage* (Maryknoll, N.Y.: Orbis Books, 1992). References will indicate paragraph numbers of the documents, except for *Justice in the World* which, in the O'Brien and Shannon book, does not number paragraphs. In this case, references will indicate page numbers.

4. I borrow the expression "deep theory" from Drew Christiansen who, in turn, borrowed it from Ronald Dworkin, *Taking Rights Seriously* (Cambridge: Harvard University Press, 1977). See Drew Christiansen, "On Relative Equality: Catholic Egalitarianism After Vatican II," *Theological Studies* 45 (1984): 668.

5. In this paper I distinguish between migrants and refugees as follows: Migrants are people who voluntarily leave one setting and move to another. The prefixes "e" and "im" before *migrant* designate migrants from the vantage point of the place of departure or arrival. Refugees are a subgroup of migrants who flee a place involuntarily because their homeland is no longer inhabitable.

6. For abbreviations used in citing ecclesial documents see the list below.

7. Janssens adopts this term from an expression found in the official record of the sessions of Vatican II.

8. John Paul II uses the terms *attitude* and *virtue* synonymously and interchangeably in relation to solidarity.

ABBREVIATIONS

The following abbreviations are used to indicate the encyclicals and synod documents:

RN: *Rerum Novarum: The Condition of Labor* (Leo XIII, 1891)

QA: *Quadragesimo Anno: After Forty Years* (Pius XI, 1931)

MM: *Mater et Magistra: Christianity and Social Progress* (John XXIII, 1961)

PT: *Pacem in Terris: Peace on Earth* (John XXIII, 1963)

GS: *Gaudium et Spes: Pastoral Constitution on the Church in the Modern World* (Second Vatican Council, 1965)

PP: *Populorum Progressio: On the Development of Peoples* (Paul VI, 1967)

OA: *Octagesimo Adveniens: A Call to Action on the Eightieth Anniversary of Rerum Novarum* (Paul VI, 1971)

JW: *Justice in the World* (Synod of Bishops, 1971)

DM: *Dives in Misericordia: Rich in Mercy* (John Paul II, 1980)

LE: *Laborem Exercens: On Human Work* (John Paul II, 1981)

SRS: *Sollicitudo Rei Socialis: On Social Concern* (John Paul II, 1987)

CA: *Centesimus Annus: On the Hundredth Anniversary of Rerum Novarum* (John Paul II, 1991)

EV: *Evangelium Vitae: The Gospel of Life* (John Paul II, 1995)

REFERENCES

Baum, G. and R. Ellsberg, eds. *The Logic of Solidarity: Commentaries on Pope John Paul II's Encyclical "On Social Concern."* New York: Orbis Books, 1989.

Bilgrien, Marie Vianney, S.S.N.D. "Collaboration—The Act that Births the Virtue of Solidarity." *New Theology Review* 8 (November 1995): 98–104.

Blume, Rev. Michael A., SVD. "Catholic Church Teachings and Documents Regarding Immigration: Theological Reflection on Immigration." In *Who Are My Sisters And Brothers?* 9–23. Washington, D.C: United States Catholic Conference, 1996.

Boland, Vivian, O.P., "Mater Et Magistra." In *The New Dictionary of Catholic Social Thought*, ed. Judith A. Dwyer, 579–590. Collegeville, Minnesota: The Liturgical Press, 1994.

Camp, Richard L. "The Rights and Duties of Labor and Capital." In *Readings in Moral Theology No. 5: Official Catholic Social Teaching*, eds. Charles E. Curran and Richard A. McCormick, S.J., 32–50. New York: Paulist Press, 1986.

————. *The Papal Ideology of Social Reform: A Study in Historical Development, 1878–1967*. Leiden, England: E. J. Brill, 1969.

Campbell-Johnston, M. "The Social Teaching of the Church." *Thought* (Autumn 1964): 38–410.

Cahill, Edward S.J. "The Catholic Social Movement: Historical Aspects." In *Readings in Moral Theology No. 5: Official Catholic Social Teaching*, 3–31.

Christiansen, Drew S.J. "Sacrament of Unity: Ethical Issues in Pastoral Care of Migrants and Refugees." In *Today's Immigrants and Refugees: A Christian Understanding*, 81–114. Washington, D.C: United States Catholic Conference, 1988.

————. "On Relative Equality: Catholic Egalitarianism After Vatican II." *Theological Studies* 45 (1984): 651–675.

Coleman, John S.J. and Gregory Baum, eds. *Rerum Novarum: One Hundred Years of Catholic Social Teaching*. Harrisburg, Pennsylvania: Trinity Press International, 1991.

Curran, Charles E. *Catholic Moral Theology in Dialogue*. Notre Dame, Indiana: University of Notre Dame Press, 1976.

————. "The Changing Anthropological Bases of Catholic Social Ethics." In *Readings in Moral Theology No. 5: Official Catholic Social Teaching*, 188–219.

Dorr, Donal. *Option For The Poor: A Hundred Years of Catholic Social Teaching*. Maryknoll, New York: Orbis Books, 1992.

Dyck, Arthur J. *Rethinking Rights and Responsibilities: The Moral Bonds of Community*. Cleveland, Ohio: The Pilgrim Press, 1994.

Gans, Herbert J. *The War Against The Poor*. New York: Basic Books, 1995.

Gilson, Etienne, ed. *The Church Speaks to the Modern World: The Social Teachings of Leo XIII*. New York: Doubleday Image Books, 1954.

Glendon, Mary Ann. *Rights Talk: The Impoverishment of Political Discourse.* New York: The Free Press, 1991.

Himes, Kenneth R., O.F.M. "The Rights of People Regarding Migration: A Perspective from Catholic Social Teaching." In *Who Are My Sisters And Brothers?* 25–32. Washington, D.C: United States Catholic Conference, 1996.

Himes, Michael J. and Kenneth R. Himes, O.F.M. *Fullness of Faith: The Public Significance of Theology.* New York: Paulist Press, 1993.

Hing, Bill Ong. *Making and Remaking Asian America through Immigration Policy: 1850–1990.* California: Stanford University Press, 1993.

Hollenbach, David S.J. *Claims in Conflict: Retrieving and Renewing the Catholic Human Rights Tradition.* New York: Paulist Press, 1979.

Ignatieff, Michael. *The Needs of Strangers: An essay on privacy, solidarity, and the politics of being human.* New York: Viking Penguin Inc, 1984.

Janssens, L. "Artificial Insemination: Ethical Considerations." *Louvain Studies* 8 (1980–1981): 3–29.

John XXIII. "Pacem in Terris." In O'Brien, David J. and Thomas A. Shannon, *Catholic Social Thought: The Documentary Heritage*, 131–162. Maryknoll, New York: Orbis Books, 1992.

———. "Mater et Magistra," 1961. In O'Brien, David J. and Thomas A. Shannon. *Catholic Social Thought*, 84–128.

John Paul II. "Evangelium Vitae." Washington, D.C.: National Conference of Catholic Bishops, 1994.

———. "Centesimus Annus," 1991. In O'Brien and Shannon, *Catholic Social Thought,* 439–488.

———. "Sollicitudo Rei Socialis," 1987. In O'Brien and Shannon, *Catholic Social Thought*, 395–436.

———. "Laborem Exercens," 1981. In O'Brien and Shannon, *Catholic Social Thought*, 352–392.

———. "Dives in Misericordia." *Origins* 10 (December 11, 1980): 401–416.

Koernke, Theresa F. "Toward an Ethics of Liturgical Behavior." *Worship* 66 (Jan. 1992): 25–38.

Lamb, Matthew. "Solidarity." In *The New Dictionary of Catholic Social Thought,* 908–912.

Land, Philip S.J. *Catholic Social Teaching: As I Have Lived, Loathed, and Loved It.* Chicago: Loyola University Press, 1994.

Langan, John S.J. "Human Rights in Roman Catholicism." In *Readings in Moral Theology No. 5: Official Catholic Social Teaching*, 110–129.

Leo XIII. "Rerum Novarum," 1891. In O'Brien and Shannon, *Catholic Social Thought,* 14–39.

Melville, Keith, ed. *National Issues Forums, Immigration: What We Promised, Where to Draw the Line.* Dubuque, Iowa: Kendall/Hunt Publishing, 1987.

Paul VI. "Octogesima Adveniens," 1971. In O'Brien and Shannon, *Catholic Social Thought,* 265–286.

————. "Populorum Progressio," 1967. In O'Brien and Shannon, *Catholic Social Thought,* 240–262.

Pius XI. "Quadragesimo Anno," 1931. In O'Brien and Shannon, *Catholic Social Thought,* 42–80.

Sacred Congregation for Bishops. "Instruction on the Pastoral Care of People Who Migrate." In *People On The Move: A Compendium of Church Documents on the Pastoral Concern for Migrants and Refugees,* 84–97. Washington, D.C: United States Catholic Conference, 1988.

Schuck, Michael J. *That They Be One: The Social Teaching of the Papal Encyclicals 1740–1989.* Washington, D.C.: Georgetown University Press, 1991.

Synod of Bishops. Justice in the World, 1971. In O'Brien and Shannon, *Catholic Social Thought,* 288–301.

Tomasi, Silvano M. "Pastoral Action and the New Immigrants," *Origins* 21 (1992): 580–584.

Unger, Sanford. *Fresh Blood: The New American Immigrants.* New York: Simon and Schuster, 1995.

United States Catholic Conference of Bishops. *Strangers and Aliens No Longer.* Washington, D.C.: United States Catholic Conference, 1993.

Vatican Council II. "Gaudium et Spes," 1965. In O'Brien and Shannon, *Catholic Social Thought,* 166–237.

Yzermans, Vincent, ed. *The Major Addresses of Pope Pius XII,* Vols. 1 & 2. St. Paul, Minnesota: North Central Publishing, 1961.

Ward, Barbara. "Looking Back on Populorum Progressio." In *Readings in Moral Theology No. 5: Official Catholic Social Teaching,* 130–149.

Fragile Outcasts: Historical Reflections on Ministry to People with AIDS

Robert J. Wister

Sean was concerned that he would be judged harshly by parishioners influenced by the unequivocal condemnation of homosexuality by the Roman Catholic Church. While the parishioners all knew and loved Sean, I feared that the church's position would keep many away from this mass. I was wrong. The church was filling up....

The realization that Sean died of AIDS brought home to our fellow parishioners, probably for the first time, that this terrible plague was in our midst. That if Sean, someone they admired and loved, could die of AIDS, then so could others; and that they, as parents, might have to cope with the ordeal we had endured. This realization was, perhaps, the contribution Sean was destined to make to the community at large....

And, of course, we worried about his relationship with the church, which viewed homosexuality with a baleful eye. Sean was truly devout, and his faith was an important element in his life. (Hopkins, 1996, xiii–xvii)

Robert Hopkins, former CIA career officer, so described his son's funeral. Sean's pastor, Monsignor John Benson, spoke of Sean's steadfast faith and devotion in his homily:

Sean's love of God and his newfound faith was evident in the many hours of his short life which were dedicated to God and his church. He touched the lives of so many with

his compassion, his kindness, and his love. He was gentle,
but he held strong convictions.
    One of God's faithful ones has gone home to Him. We
can smile with tears that the Lord who conquered death has
called Sean home to Him. (Hopkins, 1996, xv-xvi)

Sean Hopkins, diagnosed with AIDS the day after his graduation
from Georgetown University, was supported throughout his illness by
devoted parents and friends. His parish priests ministered to him with
compassion and concern. Yet, in some ways, Sean considered himself to
be an outcast from his parish community and from his church. As close
to the church as he was, Sean had hidden his illness and his sexual orientation out of fear of rejection, and was thereby deprived of much of the
spiritual assistance that would have been invaluable to him and to his
parents and friends. Acceptance and public reconciliation came too late.

    For others, reconciliation may yet be achieved. In *Breaking the
Surface*, Olympic platform diving champion Greg Louganis writes con-
cerning advice given to him by his cousin when he first learned of his
HIV status:

[John] knew this was something out of his realm, so he suggested I go to church and talk to a priest. John belonged to a
strict Greek Orthodox church, and I was brought up Greek
Orthodox. He thought that talking to a priest would help me
deal with what was going on in my life.
    For me, talking to a priest was totally out of the ques-
tion. I don't agree with a lot of what the Greek Orthodox
Church teaches, particularly when it comes to homosexuality. I had every reason to think that if I went to talk to a priest,
he'd want to talk to me about "my sin" and tell me that it was
never too late to "repent." I had nothing to repent for.
    I told John I'd think about the priest—knowing full
well that I had no intention of going. (Louganis, 1995, 187)

All persons who know they are afflicted with a terminal illness are
anxious about the days to come and search for meaning in their suffering. Dying is something all human beings have in common. It cuts
through all the things that keep us separate. Yet men and women of various ages and walks of life dying of AIDS are often rejected by family, by

friends, by clergy. Their isolation may be the product of overt and delib-
erate actions. It can also result from the person with AIDS' perception
that they have been cast out of the church and will be rejected by the
church's ministers.

A. Acknowledging the Other

A believer in the Judaeo-Christian tradition is called to accept and
respect all persons for they are created "in the image of God" (Gn 1:27).
As such, their very being encompasses a natural and supernatural likeness to God, their spiritual qualities and capabilities, their external or corporeal form, their whole person. (See the chapter by James Scullion.)
Acceptance of and respect for the worth and dignity of another person is
most perfectly achieved through personal encounter. This encounter may
have its origin in less than ideal circumstances. It may first occur in an
atmosphere tainted with pride and judgment mixed with hostility and
fear. Only when pride is displaced by humility and judgment by acceptance can the hostility and fear vanish. Then acceptance of and respect for
the other as a fellow sojourner on the earth and as a fellow child of God
follows inexorably. Encounter does not always have a positive outcome.
A sense of superiority, moral, intellectual, or physical, often leads us to
judge others to be lesser beings. This judgment can lead to acts of hostility, physical and psychological, that often are motivated by our terror at
recognition in others of our own imperfections. Made to feel inferior,
they often assimilate out of fear of discovery. They become invisible.
Once invisible, they can be ignored. It is as if they do not exist. When this
happens, those who should be brothers and sisters become outcasts.

The church, through its role as mother and teacher and in its pastoral imitation of Christ, over the centuries has reminded us that we are
created in God's image and that all people share a common heritage,
which we might call our "human dignity." Sometimes its teaching has
been applied, sometimes it goes unheeded. Sometimes, the response is
mixed. Quite often it is late. Sometimes pastoral action is stimulated by
magisterial exhortation; sometimes it is inspired simply by the example
of Christ lived out by individuals and groups of believers. Sometimes it
is effective, sometimes it is not.

B. Lessons of History

History gives us many stories of success and failure. History can teach, it can give us an understanding of why the world is as it is, why what we seek is often not what we achieve. Our lives today are touched by the decisions and actions of those who have gone before. The history of the church can help us understand why some of the most fragile among us, the dying, in particular those dying of AIDS, are considered by many and often consider themselves outcasts from the pastoral concern of the church.

The struggle to overcome judgment and fear and recognize human dignity can be shown in the stories of the oppression of the indigenous[1] American peoples. In the Americas, actions and decisions of popes, kings, clergy, and conquerors have influenced the course of the lives of countless native Americans and how the rest of the population have viewed and treated them. It is a story mixed with heroes and villains, triumphs and tragedies. It is an account of the failure of legislation, religious and civil, that did not penetrate the hearts of the powerful. It is also the story of individuals, who, inspired by the spiritual foundations of law and their personal encounters, fought for and ministered to the outcasts of this hemisphere. Perceived as outcasts themselves by many of their contemporaries, they lived out their understanding of the message of the Scriptures and laid the foundations for the concept of international law guaranteeing human rights.

The chronicle of Catholic healthcare in the United States gives us an illustration of another style of encountering, welcoming, and ministering to the outcast. Millions have been touched by the ministry of Catholic healthcare personnel. Concerned and caring persons created many institutions and opened their doors to all. They saw people in need and, without waiting for legislation or exhortation, responded and addressed the need.

Reflection on the struggle to recognize the human nature of the indigenous peoples of the Americas shows us how they became outcasts in their own land. Consideration of the ministry of Catholic healthcare illustrates care for the sick, regardless of the stigma of their illness or its origin.

Today, our society is divided by the AIDS epidemic, a crisis in which the afflicted are often looked upon through lenses tinted with judgment and fear. Ecclesiastical legislation and exhortations to address the physical and spiritual necessities of persons with AIDS often are ignored. Even when they are implemented, many of those most in need are neglected or are simply overlooked. But they are not forgotten. There are dedicated people who minister to persons with AIDS, who heed exhortations to imitate the compassion of Christ, overcome societal barriers, and encounter the outcast. Among them are the men and women of Chrysalis Ministry who encourage persons with AIDS to rediscover and recognize the spirit of God in their lives.

I. THE HUMAN NATURE OF THE INDIGENOUS PEOPLE OF THE AMERICAS

Church teachings on questions of human dignity often follow societal developments rather than lead. Pope Gregory XVI's *In Supremo Apostolatus Fastigio* condemned the slave trade only in 1839. Pope Leo XIII's social encyclical, *Rerum Novarum,* was written in 1891 after industrialization had created an urban proletariat, many of whom had abandoned a church that they perceived to be indifferent to their lot. Even when the church has taken the lead and pointed the way to recognizing and embracing the dignity of all persons, her words are not heard by many of her members. Yet individual Christians often will transcend barriers, civil and ecclesiastical, in the struggle for human dignity.

The 1992 observance of the quincentenary of Columbus's first voyage to the Americas unleashed an avalanche of books, articles, and movies. The role of the church in the conquest and evangelization of this hemisphere was subjected to close scrutiny and often scathing criticism. A reflection on the stated intentions of the rulers of Spain who funded Columbus's voyage and the official position of the Holy See reveals a stark contrast between the church's teaching on and concern for the human dignity of the indigenous peoples of the Americas and the effects of the conquest.

A. Catholic Spain in the New World

The "discovery" of the Americas in 1492 and the exploitation of these new lands and their inhabitants ignited a series of political, theological, and pastoral debates. Less than a year later, in his papal bull

Inter caetera Pope Alexander VI granted almost all of these lands to the "Catholic Kings" of Spain. This he did in the hope that they would "bring the worship of our Redeemer and the profession of the Catholic faith to their residents and inhabitants" (Ellis, 1–3).

Concern for evangelization was shared by Isabella the Catholic, Queen of Castile. In the codicil to her will she urged her husband Ferdinand, "My Lord, the King, and...the Princess, my daughter, and the Prince, her husband...[that they] neither consent nor yield to any action whereby the Indians, natives and inhabitants...suffer any harm in their persons or goods. Rather, they should command that they be treated well and justly" (Poole, 357).

Her concern was warranted. The activities of the early *conquistadores* provoked Dominican missionary friars to complain to Pope Paul III that the inhabitants of the Americas were being enslaved and their possessions confiscated. Some of the Spaniards claimed that the native peoples had no rights because they were not fully human beings. Others did not bother to adduce any reasons for their rapacity. In 1537, reports of missionary friars who lived with and had come to know the American peoples induced Pope Paul III to issue the bull *Sublimus Dei,* which affirmed the spiritual equality and human dignity of all peoples. He affirmed that "The Sublime God had so loved the human race that he has made man in such a way that not only would he share in goodness like other creatures but also that he should be able to attain that highest and inaccessible good and know it by face-to-face vision." Paul condemned, as inspired by "the enemy of the human race," those who treated the peoples of the Americas as "dumb brutes created for our service, pretending that they are incapable of receiving the Catholic faith." He affirmed that "the Indians are truly men and that they are not only capable of understanding the Catholic faith but...desire exceedingly to receive it" (Ellis, 7–8).

Paul III put teeth into his exhortation, imposing on anyone who might "presume to enslave the aforesaid Indians or despoil them of their property in any way whatsoever the pain of automatic excommunication." Pressured by the Spanish king, Emperor Charles V, Paul issued another bull the following year, revoking the censures and penalties imposed on those who defied *Sublimus Dei,* but did not take back what he had said concerning the humanity of the native peoples or their capability for conversion. This turnabout hampered the efforts of those seeking justice and was the basis for the interventions of Francisco de Vitoria and Bartolomé de Las Casas.

B. The Theological Debate over Human Rights

A debate on the nature of the conquered peoples and their rights and dignity subsequently raged throughout the Hispanic world for an entire century, becoming the first full-fledged modern debate on human rights. This debate involved the papacy, the Spanish Crown, missionaries, theologians, and lawyers.

The primary academic defender of the Conquest was Juan Ginés de Sepúlveda, a Cordovan theologian who argued on Aristotelian grounds that the enslavement of the Indians was just. Why? Because they were inferior to Spaniards, just as children were to adults, women to men, and even as apes were to humans. He likened their society to a "colony of ants." As such, the Indians legitimately could be conquered by "civil men" from Europe, and all their goods could be put to civilized use (Fuentes, 1992, 134).

1. Francisco de Vitoria

Francisco de Vitoria, a Dominican professor of theology at the University of Salamanca, responded by denouncing Francisco Pizarro's conquest of Peru. He accused the first conquistadors of invasion and aggression, and refuted the theological arguments that had been proffered to justify the repressive policy of the conquest. His lectures and writings and those of his associates created what came to be known as the School of Salamanca.

The School of Salamanca denounced the Conquest with appeals to the *Real Consejo de las Indias* and, after Vitoria's death, took their cause to the Council of Trent (1545–1563) in order to underscore the responsibility of the Crown and the Holy See in this matter. Their method and their goal was to reconcile the social and political life of the conquistadors with their Christian faith. They argued that since the Holy See and the Spanish Crown had announced that their primary intention was the conversion of the Indians, both Spain and the Catholic Church must consider the Indians to be human beings. Yet the Indians were treated without respect as if they were not truly human. Vitoria first established the humanity of the Indians as subjects for conversion. He then demonstrated that any true conversion required respect for their freedom, the teaching of that freedom, and religious instruction in the context of that freedom. It was on these premises that Vitoria and his School asserted a new legal and theological doctrine of human rights (Vicente, 1991, 7–13).

One of Vitoria's central concerns was to reinforce Aquinas' argument that all rights were natural and the consequences of God's natural law, not of God's grace. He challenged Wycliff, Hus, Luther, and other reformers, who made human rights dependent on God's grace (Vitoria, 1991, xvi, 32–42). In the reformers' view, only the "elect of God," the "saved," were entitled to these rights. Vitoria affirmed that "Every Indian is a man and thus capable of attaining salvation or damnation," that "by natural law, all men are born equal," that "every man has the right to truth, to education, and to all that forms part of his cultural and spiritual development and advancement," and that "every man has the right to his personal reputation, honor, and dignity" (Vicente, 1991, 17–19).

Vitoria asked his students if they would like to see Spaniards treated by Indians in Spain the way Spaniards treated Indians in America. He challenged them to see themselves as the oppressed, the outcast. Discovery and conquest, he said, gave Spain no more right to American territory than the Indians would possess had they discovered and conquered Spain. Although he conceded that the *status quo* of Spanish rule could not be reversed, through his books and teachings he internationalized the problem of power over the colonies and of the human rights of conquered peoples. He attempted to set down rules limiting colonial power through international law, then called *ius gentium,* or the rights of peoples (Vitoria, 1991, 277–91).

As this debate was going on in Spain, many friars in the Americas lived among the people, learned native customs and languages and treated them with compassion and humanity. Most eminent among these was Fray Bartolomé de Las Casas, Bishop of Chiapas.

2. Bartolomé de Las Casas

Bartolomé de Las Casas was a slave owner in Cuba who, after wrestling with his conscience, renounced his possessions and joined the Dominicans in 1524, accusing the conquistadors of "endless crimes and offenses against the Indians who were the king's subjects" (Fuentes, 1992, 130). Until his death in 1566, Father, later Bishop, de Las Casas denounced the injustices of the Conquest particularly the *encomienda,* a system whereby land was given to the conquistadors and the service and tribute of the Indians was required, in exchange for protection and the salvation of their souls through religious indoctrination. In reality, it was a disguised form of slavery. Las Casas's principal demands were incorporated into the Law of the Indies in 1542 (Sullivan, 1995, 248–52). The *encomienda* was legally abolished, although it remained, disguised as *repartimientos,* the "provisional" allotment of Indian laborers to the colonists.

Las Casas lamented that "so many laws...so many decrees, so many harsh threats and so many statutes conscientiously enacted by the Emperor Charles and his predecessors have been ineffective in preventing so many thousands of men from perishing by sword." Even "the fear of God and the dread of hell have not even moderated the utterly ruthless and cruel spirits of the Spaniards." Nor were the colonists tempered by "the outcries of preachers and holy men that they were barred from the sacraments of the Church and were not forgiven in sacramental confession" (Poole, 1992, 18).

Las Casas had overcome his own attitude of superiority over the native peoples and had freed his slaves. He recognized their humanity and respected their rights. Vitoria used his intellectual genius to speak for the oppressed. Las Casas and Vitoria applied the gospel and the law to a contemporary crisis. They were unafraid to take risks and were themselves regarded as outcasts by many. In spite of their efforts and the exhortations and legislation of popes and kings, in spite of the penalties, civil and ecclesiastical, connected to their laws, the human rights of the Indians were ignored by the majority of the conquistadors and by their descendants for centuries. The spirit of the gospel and the law did not "trickle down." Even the successful revolutions against Spanish rule in the nineteenth century did not bring equality to the Indian population of the Americas. This is exemplified by the 1994 Zapatista uprising in Mexico, ironically centered in Chiapas, de Las Casas's diocese. In most of Latin America, human rights and human dignity remain to this day distant dreams. Hundreds of millions remain on the margins of society, outcasts.

II. CATHOLIC HEALTHCARE IN THE UNITED STATES

In reality, ministry seldom "trickles down," unless we consider that it "trickles down" from the Scriptures. Rather, it grows out of the necessity to meet human needs in the spirit of the gospel. The development of organized healthcare under church auspices is not impelled by legislation, either ecclesiastical or civil. It well can be described as a "grass-roots" ministry.

The Greeks and Romans viewed human dignity as linked to citizenship or to virtue and responded to illness with "civic philanthropy" rather than charity based on love. In the Judaeo-Christian tradition the care of the sick is based on the belief that all are made in the image and likeness of God. The Catholic tradition urges Christians to view the sick person as an *alter Christus*. St. Vincent dePaul said to the early Daughters of Charity: "When you leave your prayers for the bedside of a patient, you are leaving God for God. Looking after the sick is praying" (Kauffman, 1995, 59).

From the earliest years of the church we find noble women such as Phoebe, Paula, and Fabiola caring for the sick poor on the fringes of society. After Christianity achieved legal status, institutions for the sick, the stranger, and the homeless were established, often under monastic auspices. The most notable early hospital was founded by Basil the Great in 372 in Caesarea in his diocese in Cappadocia (Kauffman, 1995, 14).

A. Healthcare for All

In the United States, the pluralistic character of society encouraged openness to the nation's cultural diversity and broke many of the barriers among various groups. This openness was exemplified in the policies of the many communities of religious women and men engaged in healthcare. For many years general anti-Catholic hostility was manifest in all aspects of social services. Putatively community hospitals forbade Catholic priests from entering to minister to their parishioners. While this bias tended to push many Catholics into a defensive and preservationist attitude, most Catholic healthcare facilities offered their services to all regardless of religious belief (Kauffman, 1995, 69). They respected the faith of their patients as well as their lack of faith. The *Catholic Almanac of 1850–1851* described the policy of the Sisters of

Charity's St. John's Infirmary in Milwaukee as permitting "no clergy-
man, whether Protestant or Catholic...to preach to, to pray aloud before,
or interfere religiously with such patients [who did not]...ask for the
exercise of his office." [With all patients] "the rights of conscience must
be paramount to all others" (Kauffman, 1995, 75). At the Alexian Brothers hospital in Chicago, "any sick person who desires the solace of his
religion can ask for any representative of this faith...whether they be a
Protestant preacher, a Catholic priest, a Jewish rabbi or a deacon of the
Mormon church" (Kauffman, 1995, 134). An advertisement for a hospital of the Oregon Sisters of Providence (1882) stated that "no one,
whether Jew or Gentile, Protestant or Catholic has ever been turned
away from its doors, but all have been welcomed, whether or not they
have had the means wherewith to pay" (Kauffman, 1995, 103). In the
words of Mother Alfred Moes, foundress of the Sisters of St. Francis of
Rochester, who worked with the Drs. Mayo: "The cause of suffering
humanity knows no religion or sex; the charity of the Sisters of St. Francis is as broad as their religion" (Kauffman, 1995, 132). Mother Moes's
attitude finds an echo in Pope John Paul II's definition of solidarity as a
commitment to the common good because each is responsible for all.
(See the chapter by Patricia Lamoureux.)

1. Cholera and God's Judgment

Such broad-minded attitudes were not universal. During the
cholera epidemics of the mid-nineteenth century, the *Western Sunday
School Messenger* offered the following explanation for the epidemic:
"*Drunkards and filthy wicked people of all descriptions,* are swept
away in *heaps,* as if the Holy God could no longer bear their wicked-
ness, just as we sweep away a mass of filth when it has become so corrupt we cannot bear it....The cholera is not caused by intemperance and
filth, in themselves, but it is a *scourge,* a *rod* in the hand of God" (Kauffman, 1995, 53).

Traditional clergymen said that God did not cause cholera, but it
was nonetheless symbolic of divine displeasure. "Enlightened" ministers stressed humanity's violations of the laws of nature, that is, living in squalor, as the primary cause. They were predisposed to believe
that supernatural and natural forces were responsible for the pestilence. The inherent danger of such opinions became clear when Balti-

more Archbishop James Whitfield asked, "Who does not see in this plague the finger of God?" A few months later he contracted cholera but survived the ordeal (Kauffman, 1995, 53–54). Cincinnati Bishop John Baptist Purcell more compassionately wrote, "The mysterious disease falls with particular heaviness on the poor, of whom, always, everywhere the great majority of God's elect are composed." While seeing some form of divine chastisement in the plague, rather than blaming the poor for their poverty, Purcell saw "oppression and insensibility to the wants and claims of the poor" as one of the sins that might have brought on the pestilence (Kauffman, 1995, 61).

2. Caring for People

Today, in Catholic hospitals and healthcare facilities, Catholics and many who are not Catholics minister to the physical, mental, emotional, and spiritual needs of people representing the entire spectrum of religious and secular traditions. The very nature of healthcare directs its focus to the person and the illness, without judging the worthiness of the person or the origin of the illness. In fact, each person is deemed worthy of care on the basis of their need and human dignity. For Catholics, it is Christ himself to whom they minister. Catholic healthcare evokes an activist spirituality based on a positive appreciation of human experience. Although there have been prejudices in the past and even today there is a tendency in many areas to draw clear boundaries along denominational lines, the inherently public character of healthcare fosters an accommodation to religious pluralism. Catholic healthcare, while respecting the faith of each person, nonetheless treats the entire person, recognizing their spiritual as well as their physical needs.

AIDS is the cholera epidemic of the twentieth century. Persons with AIDS are often treated like the "filthy and wicked people" denounced a hundred years ago for contracting cholera. Some see their illness as the "Scourge of God." Others, such as Bishop Purcell, are more compassionate. The impact of the AIDS epidemic can be measured in many ways, not the least of which is the church's response to persons with AIDS.

III. THE CHURCH AND AIDS

The church's response to the AIDS epidemic has been reasonably swift, given the wider community's reticence to deal with the disease. In 1983, Dr. Kevin Cahill, personal physician to Terence Cardinal Cooke, accused organized medicine of a "curious conspiracy of silence" that ended only when it became clear that the virus could go beyond the gay and Haitian communities and infect the general population (cited in Kayal, 1993, xvii). In *Called to Compassion and Responsibility* (1989, I.1), the bishops of the United States acknowledge their own "responsibility to reach out with compassion to those exposed to or experiencing this disease (AIDS) and to stand in solidarity with them and their families." The church's outreach has been laudable at many levels. Dioceses have established programs providing spiritual and physical care for persons with AIDS, opened and maintained hospices for persons with AIDS, implemented HIV education programs, and published documents that address the issue of HIV infection and its prevention. Numerous parish volunteer groups and individual Catholics have made significant efforts in caring for those with HIV and have developed new and effective services for those who are ill and for their caregivers.

This should not be surprising. Christians learn the meaning of compassion from the model of Jesus. He gives sight to the blind and makes the crippled walk; he touches and heals lepers; he shares a meal with people considered legally impure; he shames the judges of the adulterous woman and forgives her sin. With true compassion, Jesus breaks through the barriers of sickness and sinfulness in order to encounter and heal the afflicted. He tells us that he is present in the suffering, for "as you did it to one of the least of these my brethren, you did it to me" (Mt 25:40).

A. Barriers to Care

Concerning HIV/AIDS, the church's call to compassion and responsibility meets significant obstacles. For many, persons with AIDS are distant, unfamiliar people, the objects of our mingled pity and aversion, kept as far as possible from our consciousness. Pope John Paul II described persons with AIDS as facing "the challenge not only of their sickness but also the mistrust of a fearful society that instinctively turns away from them" (*Urbi et Orbi,* Christmas 1988). He assures them that "God loves you all, without distinction or limit....He loves those of you who are sick, those who are suffering from AIDS and from AIDS-related complex" (John Paul II, 1987, Mission Dolores, San Francisco, in *Unity in the Work of Service,* 185).

However, God's love must be expressed through human mediation. As St. John wrote: "If any one says, 'I love God,' and hates his brother, he is a liar; for he who does not love his brother whom he has seen cannot love God whom he has not seen" (1 Jn 4:20). Many in our society are denied compassion and love because their sexual orientation elicits unfavorable and hostile social responses, vocal disapproval and condemnation. Others are rejected because of their addiction to drugs. They are stigmatized. In classical Greek, the word *stigma* meant an actual physical mark, cut or burned into a person's skin, designating the individual's particular defect or offense. By this bodily sign, the rest of society could recognize the identity of the disgraced, the infamous, or the flawed person and avoid contact with such undesirable people. In practice in America today, a person who is stigmatized is perceived as abnormal and deviant, and thereby is dehumanized. The impact of stigma extends beyond the person so marked. It affects the person's family, friends, and business associates as well as those professionals who are involved with the stigmatized individual.

To counter this the bishops teach that "the Church holds that all people, regardless of their sexual orientation, are created in God's image and possess a human dignity which much be respected and protected" (*Called to Compassion,* 1990, IV.1). They ask that "The Christian community...provide [homosexual persons] with a special degree of pastoral understanding and care" (*To Live in Christ Jesus,* 1976, n. 9). They define the Catholic response to persons with AIDS as one in which "we discover Christ in them and they in turn are able to encounter Christ in us. Although this response undoubtedly arises in the context of religious faith, even those without faith can and must *look beyond suffering to see the human dignity and goodness of those who suffer*" (Called to Compassion, 1990, VI.1; italics added).

The Catholic response, to be complete, must provide spiritual support. While spiritual support is implied in care and in compassion, the specific spiritual needs of those suffering, the profound questions about meaning, identity, individual and communal destiny, transcendence, reconciliation, love, God, must be addressed. This is the deeper meaning of Pope Paul VI's words concerning human hope: "It is indeed in the midst of their distress that our fellowmen need to know joy, to hear its song" (Paul VI, *On Christian Joy,* 1975, n. 8).

In spite of these exhortations, many people with AIDS cannot find the necessary spiritual support at this crucial time of their lives. It is offered but many of those in need are unable to accept it in the manner and in the name in which it is offered. Because most of the church's calls for compassion are linked with reiteration of the condemnation of homosexual activity, most gays feel that they are "outside the pale" of the church's concern. Because AIDS is linked in the minds of many with homosexuality, the religious condemnation of homosexuality unwittingly prepared a context in which persons with AIDS are considered, and often consider themselves, as rejected by the church. To encounter them and to affirm their and our own human dignity we must reach out to them.

B. Ministry and the AIDS Epidemic

In the history of medicine, AIDS is without effective parallel. It is a disease that has exposed some of the flaws in our social fabric. Likewise, it has produced new challenges to pastoral care that require innovative responses. Having a severely stigmatizing disease, persons with AIDS fear discovery, discrimination, rejection, and abandonment. Jansenism in Catholicism and the growth of puritan and fundamentalist groups in Protestantism leads to a tendency to strictness and a pastoral practice that is rigorist and judgmental of persons who do not measure up. In spite of the best intentions of some pastoral leaders, feelings of alienation prevent many persons with AIDS from availing themselves of spiritual resources.

Persons in high-risk groups, especially gays and intravenous drug users, experience double jeopardy. Not only are they members of groups that have marginal social acceptability, but now they are stigmatized further by a lethal, infectious disease. Family, friends, healthcare professionals, and clergy may directly or indirectly withdraw from them at a time when they are most in need. Physical and emotional distancing is experienced by persons with AIDS as abandonment and rejection. Associated in the experience of some people with AIDS is the perception that they have been rejected by the church. Some public religious figures have suggested that AIDS is a God-sent plague, his revenge on persons who have chosen to live certain lifestyles. The United States bishops categorically "reject the idea that this illness is a direct punishment by God" (*Called to Compassion*, 1990, VI.1) and together with other religious leaders recognize the need for a more sympathetic and accepting approach to persons affected with AIDS.

The bishops of California, in an April 1987 letter, recalled that Jesus had healed "the outcasts and the wounded of his world," and said that the church should imitate his behavior and care for those who have AIDS "without judgment or imputing blame." They called on Catholics to reach out, for "People with AIDS-ARC remind us that they are not distant or unfamiliar victims to be pitied or shunned, but persons who deserve to remain within our communal consciousness and to be embraced with unconditional love" (Smith, 1988, 22).

In June 1987, the Catholic bishops of New Jersey addressed specific pastoral needs. Their policy statement on AIDS focused on the principle relationship of the church as pastor to persons with AIDS. They recognized their obligation to provide pastoral ministry "at every stage in the disease's progression, and to...families, friends, and associates." They emphasized that "persons with AIDS shall have the rights to the sacraments and Christian burial," and that the identity of such a person is confidential and "every precaution shall be taken to maintain that confidentiality." In finding it necessary to assert these rights, the bishops acknowledged pastoral situations in which they were denied and the continuing alienation caused by callous behavior on the part of some clergy. In affirming rights to the sacraments and Christian burial, they confirmed the membership of persons with AIDS in the church. In affirming their right to confidentiality, the bishops respected their personal dignity. It is sad that these affirmations were necessary but in making them the bishops have taken a positive and constructive step toward achieving compassion and reconciliation (Smith, 1988, 22–23).

For all, reconciliation is difficult. Large numbers of persons with AIDS have been away from institutional religious practice for a number of years. During those years they have not perceived the church as a welcoming place. They consider themselves to have been "segregated out, their human value...diminished" (Kayal, 1993, 25). These perceptions do not change easily. People do not make transitions simply because they are seriously ill and are approached by a pastor or minister.

Nonetheless, many persons on the fringe of organized religion have maintained and continue to maintain a vibrant interior life. From youth they internalized the essentials of a religious heritage, maintaining a belief in God and a sense of social obligations toward other persons but cannot consider the church as a safe haven.

IV. CHRYSALIS

In the midst of such a profound sense of alienation, it is critical to uphold the value and dignity of every human person. The affirmation of Genesis 1:27 is critical—that every person is created in the image and likeness of God. In the first chapter of Genesis the human person, unlike other creatures, is defined on the basis of a relationship with God. This truth establishes the dignity and radical equality of all human beings. It is of great importance, especially for those who experience "distance" and "isolation," that any approach to spirituality be based first of all on the recognition of the unconditional love of God who gives to each person his or her individual human dignity.

Personal spirituality and the ability to address spiritual issues is an intrinsic part of human existence. Even those who do not profess a belief in God experience a "spiritual" side to their lives. In particular when confronted with life-threatening disease, the need to address spiritual issues becomes acute. Many are able to draw on resources developed over a lifetime of involvement with a church or synagogue or, at least, to seek the assistance of their faith community. Others, even those who feel part of the church, draw back. Still others have been alienated from their faith community for a variety of reasons. Often they are afraid of the judgment of the church. These persons are no less in need of spiritual assistance; in fact, they may be more in need than others who feel comfortable in church sponsored activities.

These persons are the "fragile outcasts." They have not heard or have not been able to believe church leaders urging compassion and pastoral assistance for them. Many of them are twice, three times, or even four times "outcast." They might be gay, addicted to drugs, living in poverty, as well as members of a minority community, or all of the above. Many are in the acute stage of HIV. They are physically, emotionally, financially, and spiritually fragile. Yet they are human beings who have a right to spiritual sustenance.

A. Seeing the Need

Brother Bill Stevens, after 25 years as a teaching Christian Brother, served ten years as a hospital chaplain. There he encountered AIDS. He overcame his fears of the disease and became a "buddy" to persons with AIDS. Soon after he was appointed Director of the Metuchen (N.J.) Diocese Office of Pastoral Care for AIDS. As director, he established various programs, including retreats. However, he soon discovered that many in need would not attend these retreats because they were church-sponsored. He realized that too much identification with the Catholic Church, or any church for that matter, caused many to hesitate and to stay away. He then established the *Chrysalis Ministry*[2] to provide non-denominational retreats for people with AIDS. Chrysalis also provides other services such as luncheon outreach and individual support. Since most retreatants have been impoverished by the medical costs of the disease and are unemployed, the retreats are free. Brother Bill finances them with funding from the Christian Brothers, small gifts, and the contributions he receives from an appeal through the mail. The original mailing list was the roster of the Catholic diocesan priests of New Jersey. They remain the chief source of contributions.

1. A Space for Transformation

Four-day retreats are held three to four times per year, each with 50–60 participants. Retreats are open to all: black/white, poor/very poor, professional/homeless, gay/straight, men/women, all races and creeds. One goal of the retreat is to "establish a safe and nurturing space" that will enable people to get in touch with their spiritual resources—whatever this might be for them. Retreatants are forbidden to have or use drugs or alcohol and are enjoined to "show respect and/or acceptance of those attending...without regard to race, sexual orientation or life styles." Any retreatant who "disregards the attempts to build a support-ive community by engaging in exclusive relationships" will be asked to leave the retreat (Chrysalis Mission Statement).

Chrysalis purposefully abstains from "power politics" in its response to the AIDS crisis. It eschews alliance with gay rights organi-zations or with church-affiliated gay groups. One reason for this is that many of the retreatants are not gay. The ministry's focus is on the disease and assisting the people infected with it. We may say, however, that Chrysalis is "political" in a way. Chrysalis practices a "politics of transformation." Its ministers simply ask what people can do and need to do together for others. In so acting, both the ministers and the persons to whom they minister are transformed.

Like most retreats, Chrysalis provides a combination of individual and group experiences and time for public and private prayer and meditation. They are usually held at a Catholic retreat center in New Jersey. While they remain non-denominational, the chapel is an oft-visited place for the retreatants and staff. Group sessions regularly include themes such as "The Mystery in Your Life," "The Healing Power of Story," "Tai-Chi Meditation," "Creative Movement," and various aspects of meditation. The community of the retreatants is bound together by their experience of AIDS, not their sexual orientation, their past lives, their race, or their creed.

The retreat team is made up of volunteers from a variety of backgrounds. They include Catholic priests, brothers and sisters, an Episcopal priest, a certified NACC woman chaplain, a woman from the Quaker tradition, a pastoral associate from a Catholic parish, registered nurses, a massage therapist, personnel from professional care-giving professions, and persons living with AIDS.

The retreat seeks to understand and accept what the person with AIDS holds as life's values. It takes time to create the proper emotional climate in which a person is willing to share on a deep personal level. Staff must not only understand each retreatant's personal values, but it is even more important for them to communicate acceptance of these values. Acceptance does not imply agreement. This is an important distinction. Some of the expressed values of persons in high risk groups will not be endorsed by some staff members. Just as professional counselors must learn to be non-judgmental in dealing with clients' values at odds with their own, so too must staff appropriate these attitudes in their ministry with persons with AIDS.

2. The People of Chrysalis

The Chrysalis staff discovered that the retreat encounter transforms them as well as the retreatants. They describe their lives as enriched. "They give us more than we give them." They find they are more able to deal better with their stressful occupations. "We don't do anything that special. I go home exhausted physically but renewed spiritually." These comments may appear simple, but their very simplicity is indicative of the mutuality of the encounter in response to pain and need. (See the chapter by Ron DiSanto.) The retreat in its entirety is a "liturgical act" in which staff and retreatants encounter God together, each in their own way. (See the chapter by Edward Foley.)

Chrysalis does not replace church-based programs. It supplements them and reaches those who "fall between the cracks," or for whom the church's concern has not "trickled down." While it reaches out to "outcasts," it does not pity them as such. One retreatant remarked that the retreat "enables me to enter the world of the living, if only for a short period of time." This is not neat and tidy, black and white, much less obviously "Catholic." Yet it is an honest attempt to respond to the biblical tradition, to the example and injunctions of Jesus, to the *Call to Compassion* of the National Conference of Catholic Bishops, to the example of Vitoria and de Las Casas, to the tradition of Catholic healthcare. It takes all of the above another step. Catholic healthcare reached out and reaches out to care for those suffering from physical illness, without regard for their race, religion, economic status, or the origin of their disease. It treats the disease and the person without any discrimination. Chrysalis reaches out to those in spiritual pain, without regard for their race, religion, economic status, or the origin of their disease. It seeks to assist them to find spiritual peace where there is spiritual conflict or emptiness.

V. CONCLUSION

Vitoria and de Las Casas affirmed the human dignity and respected the beliefs of the native peoples of the Americas. Las Casas and many friars encountered and ministered to them in spite of the attitudes, behavior, and criticism of many of their contemporaries. Chrysalis affirms the human dignity of each person, respecting their right to their faith and to their system of beliefs. Catholic healthcare focuses primarily on physical health without judging the patient or the illness. Chrysalis addresses the spiritual health of persons with AIDS without judging their lives, their beliefs, or their illness.

Church leaders have called for pastoral actions based on the principle of the human dignity of each person. I am reasonably certain that "non-denominational spiritual retreats" are not what the pope and the bishops had in mind. Yet, human dignity in its fullest sense must include the spiritual life of all persons. Chrysalis acts in the spirit called for by the bishops, nuancing their pastoral response so that they do not discourage those most in need of pastoral, of spiritual care. In so doing, Chrysalis exemplifies the best of the Catholic pastoral tradition.

The following of Jesus exemplified in this ministry may best be expressed not in the application of critical exegesis or historical analysis, but in the opening words of *The Testament of St. Francis:*

> The Lord gave me, Brother Francis, thus to begin doing penance in this way: for when I was in sin, it seemed too bitter for me to see lepers. The Lord Himself led me among them and I showed a heart full of mercy to them. When I left them, what had seemed bitter to me was turned into sweetness of soul and body. Afterwards I tarried a little and left the world.

NOTES

1. Throughout this chapter I refer to the indigenous peoples of the Americas as "Native Americans" and as "indigenous Americans." In some quotes they are called "Indians." Recognizing that all peoples have the right to name themselves, I try to use terminology that shows respect for this right and accurately reflects the sources quoted.

2. In some ways Chrysalis is modeled on Damien Ministries of Washington, D.C. Damien was founded in 1987. (http://www. catholic.net/rcc/Cnvs/programs/dami.html)

Transformation retreats, under the auspices of the Diocese of Richmond, has offered non-denominational retreats for persons with AIDS in the Commonwealth of Virginia. (http://www.views.edu/views/ hiv/transr96.html)

REFERENCES

Alexander, Marilyn Bennett, and James Preston. *We Were Baptized Too.* Louisville: Westminster John Knox Press, 1996.

Coleman, S.S., Gerald D. *Homosexuality: Catholic Teaching and Pastoral Practice.* New York: Paulist Press, 1995.

Fuentes, Carlos. *The Buried Mirror.* Boston: Houghton Mifflin Company, 1992.

Hopkins, Robert. *Sean's Legacy: An AIDS Awakening*. Ligouri, Mo.: Triumph Books, 1996.

John Paul II. *"Evangelium Vitae,"* Origins 24 (1995): 689-727.

Kauffman, Christopher. *Ministry and Meaning: A Religious History of Catholic Health Care in the United States*. New York: Crossroad, 1995.

Kayal, Philip M. *Bearing Witness: Gay Men's Health Crisis and the Politics of AIDS*. Boulder, Colo.: Westview Press, 1993.

de Las Casas, Bartolomé. *In Defense of the Indians*. Tr. Stafford Poole, C.M. DeKalb, Ill.: Northern Illinois University Press, 1992.

Louganis, Greg, with Eric Marcus. *Breaking the Surface*. New York: Random House, 1995.

National Conference of Catholic Bishops. *Called to Compassion and Responsibility—A Response to the HIV/AIDS Crisis*. Washington, D.C.: NCCB Publications, 1990; also *Origins* 19(1989): 421–34.

Paul VI. *On Christian Joy*. Washington, D.C.: USCC Office for Publication and Promotion Services, 1975.

Smith, S.J., Walter. *AIDS: Living & Dying With Hope*. New York: Paulist Press, 1988.

Sullivan, S.J., Francis Patrick. *Indian Freedom: The Cause of Bartolomé de las Casas 1484–1566*. Kansas City: Sheed & Ward, 1995.

Unity in the Work of Service: John Paul II on the Occasion of His Second Pastoral Visit to the United States. Washington, D.C.: USCC Office for Publication and Promotion Services, 1987.

Vicente, Luciano Pereña. *Derechos y Deberes Entre Indios y Españoles En El Nuevo Mundo Según Francisco de Vitoria*. Salamanca: Universidad Pontificia de Salamanca, 1991.

de Vitoria, Francisco. *Political Writings*. Eds. Anthony Pagden and Jeremy Lawrence. Cambridge: Cambridge University Press, 1991.